THE COMPLETE BOOK OF
INDIAN COOKING

THE COMPLETE BOOK OF
INDIAN COOKING

Edited by
Veronica Sperling & Christine McFadden

PARRAGON

First published in Great Britain in 1996 by
Parragon Book Service Ltd
Unit 13–17
Avonbridge Trading Estate
Atlantic Road
Avonmouth
Bristol BS11 9QD

ISBN: 0-75252-056-3 (hbk)
ISBN: 075252-003-2 (pbk)

Printed in Italy

Produced by Haldane Mason, London

Acknowledgements
Art Direction: Ron Samuels
Design: Digital Artworks Partnership Ltd

Material contained in this book has previously appeared in
Classic Indian Cooking and *Indian Side Dishes* by Cara Hobday
Quick & Easy Indian Cooking and *Indian Vegetarian Cooking* by Louise Steele
Balti Cooking by Jenny Beresford
Recipes with Yogurt by Pamela Westland

Contents

INTRODUCTION 6

APPETIZERS 18

FISH DISHES 44

POULTRY DISHES 70

MEAT DISHES 96

VEGETABLE DISHES 122

RICE DISHES 162

PULSE DISHES 188

BREADS 208

CHUTNEYS, PICKLES
& RELISHES 224

DESSERTS 236

INDEX 254

INDIAN CUISINE

The cuisine of India offers a whole range of mouthwatering recipes to the adventurous cook. Every region of this vast nation has its own favourite ingredients, flavourings and methods of cooking, and the variety of dishes is extensive. This book contains a complete collection of recipes for all tastes and occasions. Whether you want a quick and easy meal or a complete Indian-style dinner, you'll find everything you need, right down to the appetizers and drinks, to capture the flavour of India.

INDIAN REGIONAL COOKING

With India's vast geographical range and varied natural resources, cooking is highly regional. In the past, difficult transportation meant that cooks could not obtain fresh ingredients from other parts of the country, so local dishes developed, making the most of available produce. The number of religions throughout India also has a strong influence on food and cooking, as each has its own strict dietary code.

The diversity of Indian cuisine is most obvious in the contrast between the rich, meat-based dishes served with bread in the northern states of Punjab, Kashmir and Uttar Pradesh, and the spicy-hot, pulse-based vegetarian cuisine of the south, where rice is the staple accompaniment.

Northern India

Even today, food from the north reflects the influence of Muslim Moguls who conquered India in the sixteenth century. The invaders brought with them a love of good living and rich Persian recipes for fragrant and flavourful rice dishes, such as the nut and fruit pilaus and the saffron-flavoured meat and rice casseroles called biryanis. Mogul courts located in northern cities became the sites of lavish banquets and great feasts; gold and silver platters were piled high with mounds of subtly flavoured and beautifully coloured foods, garnished with thin leaves of pounded silver called vark. This legacy lives on, in that the food prepared for today's great celebrations – weddings, births, family gatherings – will be mogul-style dishes.

Other popular dishes that reflect the Mogul influence, both locally and on Indian restaurant menus around the world, include kormas – braised meat in creamy sauces, and koftas – spicy meatballs that are grilled (broiled), then slowly cooked in rich sauces. Dishes from these areas often include the words mughlai and shahi in their titles. Mughlai food is spicy and rich, as it is traditionally cooked in ghee. Cream and almonds are regular ingredients in these dishes. The southern city of Hyderabad is an exception to the north/south divide as the richness of northern-style Mogul cooking continues here today.

Punjab is also the home of tandoori dishes, where marinated meat and seafood are cooked in clay ovens called tandoors which are positioned over charcoal or wood-burning fires. Tandoori chicken is probably the best-known tandoori dish, but leavened naan breads are also cooked on the sides of the oven. Modern homes rarely include tandoori ovens, so the grill (broiler) or outdoor barbecue are more commonly used. Purists say the results are not the same, but the food is still dry on the outside and tender and succulent inside.

Large numbers of Indians living in the north of the country are Hindus, to whom the cow is sacred, so beef is rare. Fragrant long-grain basmati rice, grown in the foothills of the Himalayas, forms the basis of the pilaus and biryanis.

Southern India

Rice is served with every meal in the southern regions of India, and as it doesn't grow there, it has to be transported from the north. Rice is used to absorb the characteristic liquid-style curries and is served with pulse-based dishes to provide protein – vital in an area which is overwhelmingly vegetarian.

In the hot and humid eastern plains that surround Bengal, the mustard plant flourishes, providing oil for

cooking and spicy seeds for flavouring. Rice and seafood appear in many meals, often flavoured with mustard oil.

Seafood, coconut and fresh chillies are cooked in endless combinations in the western coastal regions around Goa. This is the home of the ultra-hot vindaloo curries, given a distinctive hot and sour flavour by local chillies and vinegar. Christian communities were established here when the region was conquered by the Portuguese, and their influence means that pork vindaloos are found, unlike areas with large Muslim or Hindu populations. The region is also the home of 'Bombay Duck'. Neither from Bombay nor a duck, it is a small fish that is dried in the sun and sold in thin strips.

In hot Madras and the surrounding southern states, highly spiced grains and lentils make up a substantial part of the daily diet, with rice and lentils often combined in a single dish. Meals also include a selection of the lush exotic fruit that thrive in the hot, tropical climate. Bananas are a daily snack, while the trees' large, shiny green leaves are used traditionally as serving platters instead of plates.

INDIAN MEALS

Traditionally, all the dishes in an Indian meal are served at once, without any concept of courses. Although Indian restaurants in the West follow our style of serving different courses, this is not the way in typical Indian homes, whether they are vegetarian or meat-eating families. A meal in a meat-eating home will consist of a meat dish, a vegetable dish, a pulse dish, a chutney or relish for accompaniment and, in the south, a large bowl of steaming rice or, in the north, freshly baked bread. Each of the dishes is selected to provide a harmonious blend of flavours. The meal may be served in individual bowls for the diners to help themselves, or each person may have their own thali – a large metal plate with individual bowls on it.

Creamy Indian ice–cream (kulfi), a pudding or fresh fruit may be served as a dessert. In the north as well as the south it is customary for Indians to eat with the fingers of the right hand, rather than cutlery, except possibly when entertaining Western guests. Northern diners use just their fingertips or pieces of flat, unleavened bread, such as chapatis, while southerners are quite skilled at using their whole hand. It is not acceptable to use the left hand while eating as it is considered unclean.

Indians have a sweet tooth and like to eat various sweets throughout the day, bought from special stores or on street corners. Many are brightly coloured and all are very sweet, flavoured with coconut, nuts or rose water. Such sweets are an essential part of many religious celebrations.

INDIAN DRINKS

When serving spicy dishes be sure to have plenty of refreshing drinks to hand – chilled mineral water, iced water and fruit juice are ideal. For special occasions and for a deliciously refreshing drink to sip during a hot, spicy meal, serve iced water flavoured with whole spices such as cardamom pods, cumin seeds or cinnamon sticks. Wine is generally not a very good accompaniment to an Indian meal as the taste is overpowered by the strong flavours of the food. Instead, serve chilled lagers and beers.

For a really authentic touch, serve Lassi, the deliciously cooling Indian drink of lightly spiced yogurt. Simply mix 600 ml/1 pint/2½ cups of natural yogurt with an equal quantity of water and whisk until smooth. For a sweet version, stir in 1 tsp rose water, 4 tsp caster (superfine) sugar, the crushed seeds from 4 cardamom pods and sprinkle with chopped pistachio nuts. For a savoury version, stir in ¼ tsp salt, 1 tsp sugar, ¼ tsp roasted crushed cumin seeds and garnish with fresh mint sprigs. Serve in a jug or tall glasses with plenty of crushed ice.

INGREDIENTS

It's never been easier to create quick and authentic-tasting Indian food thanks to the marvellous range of exciting spices, herbs and ready-prepared products so widely available. All the ingredients used in the recipes are easy to find in large supermarkets and Asian grocery stores.

Chillies

Much of the heat in Indian dishes comes from the use of fresh chillies, although dried and ground chillies are also commonplace in Indian kitchens. In southern India, with its searingly hot temperatures, chillies are used in copious amounts because they cause the body to perspire, which has a cooling affect. It's not surprising, therefore, that southern India is home to the fiery vindaloo curries. Numerous varieties of fresh chilli grow in India and they come in a range of sizes and intensities, from fairly mild to very hot. As a general rule, the smaller a chilli, the hotter it will be.

The heat in a chilli comes from a substance in the core and the seeds. Although most recipes specify deseeded chillies, it is really a matter of personal taste. If you do not want your dish to be too hot, cut the chilli in half lengthways and remove the seeds and core with the tip of the knife before you chop the chilli. Wear rubber gloves or wash your hands afterwards, otherwise your face, eyes or mouth will sting if you touch them.

Fresh chillies will keep for about five days in the refrigerator.

Coconut

Fresh coconut milk is unmistakable in both savoury and sweet dishes from the area around Goa and in many of the vegetarian dishes of southern India. Coconut milk and the freshly grated flesh are regularly included in rich seafood curries, and the flesh is often added to chutneys for its slightly crunchy texture as well as its flavour.

Before you buy a coconut, give it a good shake to make sure you can hear plenty of liquid sloshing around inside; the more liquid it has, the fresher it will be. Use a hammer and screw driver or the tip of a sturdy knife to poke out the three soft 'eyes' in the top, and shake out all the coconut water. Use the hammer to tap the coconut around the centre until it splits in half. Crack the coconut halves into manageable pieces, then

break away the shell. Peel off the thin brown skin. You can then grate the white coconut flesh by hand or in a food processor. The grated flesh will freeze for up to three months and can be used straight from frozen in curries and other cooked dishes.

Coconut milk and creamed coconut

When fresh coconut isn't available, these two ingredients are ideal for adding an authentic Indian flavour to sweet and savoury dishes. Coconut milk is sold in cans or as a powder which needs to be made up with water. Creamed coconut is sold in compressed bars and can be added directly to dishes, or dissolved in water first. It gives a richer flavour and texture than canned or powdered coconut milk. You can make coconut milk by soaking unsweetened desiccated (shredded) coconut in water and then straining it through muslin (cheesecloth) and squeezing out all the flavoured liquid. Do not confuse creamed coconut with coconut cream, which is a very sweet, thick, syrupy mixture used in cocktails.

Garlic

Native to India, garlic adds its sharp, distinctive flavour to dishes throughout the country, and is one of the essential ingredients of the rich Mogul dishes from northern India. It is also popular for flavouring vegetarian dishes, when it is often teamed with fresh ginger. Garlic keeps well at room temperature providing the room isn't too warm, in which case it should be stored in the refrigerator.

Ghee

Many Indian recipes specify using ghee as the cooking fat. This is because it is similar to clarified butter in that it can be heated to a very high temperature without burning. Ghee adds a nutty flavour to dishes and a glossy shine to sauces. You can buy ghee in cans, and a vegetarian version is also available. Store at room temperature or keep in the refrigerator. If it is not available, substitute a mixture of sunflower oil and butter – the oil prevents the butter from burning when heated.

Ginger

Spicy vegetarian and Mogul dishes often contain ginger for its characteristic flavour and aroma. The gnarled pale brown roots are sold in supermarkets and Asian grocery stores. Peel before use then grate or chop finely. Indian cooks often pound ginger into a paste with onions and other spices, and in Mogul cooking a classic flavouring combination is ginger, garlic and onions, often pounded together. Although ground ginger is a popular ingredient in Western baking recipes, do not substitute it for fresh ginger in savoury Indian recipes.

Gram flour

Also called besan flour, this pale yellow flour is made from ground chick-peas (garbanzo beans). In Indian kitchens it is used to make breads, bhajis and batters and to thicken sauces and stabilize yogurt when it is added to hot dishes. Buy it from Asian grocery stores or large health food stores and store in a cool, dark place in an air-tight container.

Herbs

Indian cooks use many fresh herbs to balance spicy flavours and to add freshness to dishes. To release their full flavour, fresh herbs should be bruised or chopped just before cooking.

BASIL, CORIANDER (CILANTRO), MINT AND PARSLEY are popular fresh herbs in Indian cooking. Only the leaves of basil and mint are used. However, if you're adding parsley or coriander to a dish, the finely chopped stalks as well as the leaves may be used as they also contain flavour. Coriander (cilantro) looks like flat-leaf parsley, but it has a more pronounced flavour and the two herbs are not interchangeable. When you buy fresh herbs, look for firm stalks and leaves which look like they have 'bounce' in them: limp and yellowing leaves are a sign that the herb is not fresh. To store herbs, rinse off any dirt and immerse the stems in water up to their leaves. They will keep in a cool place for up to four days. Fresh leaves can also be finely chopped and frozen in small containers so they can be used straight from the freezer.

Dried, freeze-dried and frozen herbs are great stand-bys when fresh ones aren't available. You can extract extra flavour from dried herbs if you warm them in the oven before you use them. Just spread them out on a baking sheet (cookie sheet) and place in a preheated low oven for 3–4 minutes until they become fragrant. You will be able to smell the aroma when they are ready.

Nuts

Pale green pistachios, cashews and almonds are regular ingredients in both savoury and sweet Indian cooking. The nuts are used both whole and finely ground, often as a thickener for sauces. Freshly ground nuts have the best flavour as grinding releases their natural oils, so it's best to buy nuts whole and grind them yourself, rather than using packets of ready-ground nuts.

Oils

Indian cooks use a variety of vegetable oils.

GROUNDNUT OR SUNFLOWER OIL are good for most dishes, although more specialist oils are sometimes called for.

COCONUT OIL Particularly popular in southern and western India, coconut oil is extracted from coconut flesh and has a mild taste.

MUSTARD OIL In Bengal, cooks favour this dark golden oil with a pungent flavour. It is also used in pickles throughout India.

SESAME OIL Unlike Chinese sesame oil, the Indian variety is light and colourless. Spices are often fried in it before being combined with other ingredients.

Pulses (legumes)

Dried beans, peas and lentils are an essential ingredient in Indian cooking which is renowned for its interesting and delicious range of pulse dishes, usually known as dal. Pulses are especially valuable in vegetarian homes where, combined with a grain dish and a dairy product, they provide one of the main sources of protein.

When you buy dried pulses, always check the package for any small stones or husks, and remove them before cooking. Dried pulses keep for up to six months in an air-tight container, after which the skins begin to toughen, so buy your pulses from a store with a fast turnover. Do not season pulses until after cooking as the salt may also cause them to become tough. Never overlook the option of using canned pulses, which simply need draining and rinsing before use. As canned beans and peas tend to be quite soft in texture, they are usually added to dishes towards the end of the cooking time to prevent them becoming too soft.

With the exception of lentils, all whole, dry pulses need an overnight soak before cooking. Alternatively, for a quicker method, place the pulses in a pan, cover with water, bring to the boil and boil for 10 minutes. Remove from the heat, cover and leave to soak for 3 hours. Drain and place the pulses in a clean pan, cover with fresh water and bring to the boil. Boil hard for 10 minutes, then simmer for the amount of time specified in the recipe.

This second boiling is important to kill poisonous toxins present in some pulses. The total cooking time will depend on the freshness of the pulses: the fresher they are, the quicker they will cook.

The following pulses are most frequently used in Indian cooking:

BLACK-EYED BEANS These oval-shaped beans are grey or beige with a dark dot in the centre. They have a slightly smoky flavour. They are sold canned as well as dried.

CHANNA DAL Similar to yellow split peas in appearance, they are husked and split black chick-peas (garbanzo beans). The grains are smaller and the flavour slightly sweeter than that of yellow split peas which you will also see sold as channa dal.

CHICK-PEAS (GARBANZO BEANS) Cream coloured and resembling a hazelnut in appearance, these peas have a nutty flavour and slightly crunchy texture. Indian cooks grind them to make a flour called gram or besan, which is used to make breads, to thicken sauces and to make batters for deep-fried dishes such as onion bhajis.

LENTILS As well as the familiar green-brown variety of lentils, Indians also cook a great deal with the milder flavoured split red and yellow lentils. All varieties have the advantage of not needing presoaking or boiling before cooking, which makes them the most convenient pulses to use. Be careful, however, not to over-cook lentils or their texture will be reduced to a pulpy mess.

RED KIDNEY BEANS Popular to use in spicy stews, soups and sauces, these beans have a nutty flavour and are readily available dried and canned. If using dried beans, don't forget to boil them hard for 10 minutes before simmering. This is essential to kill a poisonous enzyme they contain. Canned red kidney beans, however, do not need boiling.

Rice

Long-grain rice is an important ingredient in Indian cooking, especially for vegetarians and in southern India where bread is rarely served. Basmati rice, grown in the Himalayan foothills, has long, slender grains with a delicate flavour that sets it apart from other long-grain rices and accounts for its higher price. You can substitute American or Patna long-grain rice for basmati, but the result will not be quite as good. Easy-cook and brown versions of basmati rice are sold in supermarkets.

To cook basmati rice, put 250 g/8 oz/1½ cups of rice in a fine sieve (strainer) and rinse under cold running water until the water runs clear. Put the rice in a bowl, cover with fresh water and leave to soak for 30 minutes.

Drain the rice and transfer to a heavy-based saucepan. Add enough water to cover the rice by 2.5 cm/1 inch. Bring to the boil over a high heat then stir well. Cover the pan tightly, turn off the heat and leave for 25 minutes. Do not be tempted to lift the lid before the time is up, otherwise the steam will escape and the rice will not cook properly.

Remove the pan from the burner and leave to stand for a further 10 minutes before removing the lid. Fluff the rice with a fork and serve.

Rose water

The diluted essence extracted from rose petals is a popular ingredient in Indian desserts, and an essential flavouring of many Mogul dishes. It adds an exotic quality to drinks and sweetmeats. Only a few drops are needed to flavour a dish. You can buy it in delicatessens, supermarkets and Asian food stores.

Spices

Spices play an essential part in Indian cooking but don't let the vast array on supermarket shelves put you off. You will only need a few familiar ones to give your cooking an authentic taste. It is best to buy whole spices and grind them as needed because they keep their flavour and aroma much longer than ready-ground spices. You can grind spices with a pestle and mortar or use a spice grinder or small electric food processor kept just for that purpose. Buy your spices in small quantities and store them in a cool, dark place so they stay fresh and retain their aroma. If you do buy ground spices, however, be sure to check that they are not past the sell-by date as the flavour and fragrance will probably have deteriorated.

Indian cooks use several techniques to coax all the flavour from dried spices and give dishes well harmonized flavours that do not taste raw. One method is to dry-fry or roast whole seeds over a gentle heat. As the spices roast, they begin to jump around in the pan, so it is a good idea to use a heavy-based frying pan (skillet) with a lid. Dry-frying takes only a few minutes and you will be able to tell when the spices are ready because of the wonderful fragrance that develops. Be sure to stir the spices constantly and never take your eyes off the pan because the spices can burn very quickly.

DRY-FRIED SPICE MIX Add 1 teaspoon of this handy mixture to rice, pulses or stews during cooking to give an authentic flavour. Heat a small heavy-based frying pan (skillet) over a medium heat. When it is hot, add 4 tablespoons of coriander seeds and 1 tablespoon of cumin seeds. Fry, stirring constantly, until the seeds turn a few shades darker. You should be able to smell the aroma. Immediately pour the seeds on to a plate and leave to cool. Using a pestle and mortar or a small electric spice grinder, grind the seeds as finely as possible. The mixture will keep in an airtight container for up to one month.

Another technique is to slowly fry the spices in the ghee or vegetable oil that will be used for cooking the other ingredients. This has the advantage of not only bringing out the flavours of the various spices, but also adding spiciness to the cooking oil.

The following are the most common spices used in Indian dishes:

AJOWAN Related to caraway and cumin, these small brown seeds are valued for their digestive properties. They are used in vegetable dishes, especially in southern India, and in breads.

ANISEED Similar to fennel seeds, these small seeds are a popular ingredient in food from the Bengali and Kashmiri regions. They taste and smell similar to liquorice. They are also available ground from Indian food stores.

CARDAMOM These small pods contain numerous tiny black seeds which have a warm flavour and are highly aromatic. Green cardamoms are considered the best because of their fine, delicate flavour. Black pods make an adequate substitute, but they have a much stronger flavour. Green cardamoms are also prized for their digestive properties, and some Indians chew them raw after they have eaten extra-spicy curries, to aid digestion and sweeten the breath. Used in both sweet and savoury dishes, cardamom pods are usually lightly crushed prior to use to allow the full flavour of the seeds to be appreciated. Whole or crushed cardamom pods are not meant to be eaten, so they should be removed before serving or left on the side of the plate. Some recipes specify using just the seeds rather than the whole pod. To remove the seeds, use the end of a rolling pin or a pestle and mortar to break open the pod and take out the seeds. Ground cardamom is the finely ground pods.

CASSIA This spice comes from the bark of the cassia tree. It is similar in appearance and flavour to cinnamon but is not as uniform in shape. Cinnamon can be used in its place.

CAYENNE PEPPER Orange-red in colour, this ground pepper is extremely hot and pungent, being made from dried red chillies.

CHILLI The quickest way to add heat to a curry or other Indian dish is to add a crumbled dried red chilli, or dried chilli flakes. For extra heat add the seeds as well.

CINNAMON SHAVINGS These are obtained from the bark of the cinnamon tree and are processed and curled to form the sticks of this fragrant spice. The sticks are not edible, although they make an attractive garnish as well as adding flavour to sweet and savoury dishes. Cinnamon is also available ground.

CLOVES These dried, unopened flower buds are used to give flavour and aroma to both sweet and savoury dishes, but should be used with caution because the flavour can be overwhelming if too many are used. Whole cloves are not meant to be eaten. Cloves are one of the spices traditionally included in garam masala.

CORIANDER Available ground or as seeds, this spice is one of the essential ingredients in Indian cooking. Coriander seeds are often dry roasted before use to develop their flavour.

CUMIN These caraway-like seeds are popular with Indian cooks because of their warm, pungent flavour and aroma. The seeds are sold whole or ground, and are usually included as one of the flavourings in garam masala.

FENUGREEK The seed of this herb is used for its bitter flavour and pronounced aroma, especially in vegetarian dishes and pickles. You will find the seeds and a ground version in Indian grocery stores.

GARAM MASALA This is actually a mixture of ground spices, not an individual spice. The usual combination includes cardamom, cinnamon, cloves, cumin, nutmeg and black peppercorns, but most Indian cooks have a personal recipe, often handed down for generations. Garam masala is usually added to savoury dishes at the end of cooking so the heat doesn't destroy the subtle flavouring. You can buy prepared garam masala at large supermarkets or Asian grocery stores, or you can make your own: finely grind together 2 tbsp cumin seeds, 2 tbsp coriander seeds, 1 tbsp black peppercorns, 2 tsp cloves, 1 tsp cardamom seeds, 2 dried bay leaves, 1 cinnamon stick (about 7.5 cm/3 inches), 1 dried red chilli. Store in an airtight container and use within three weeks.

MUSTARD SEEDS These tiny, reddish-brown seeds are used throughout India, and are a particularly important ingredient in pickles and in southern vegetarian cooking. The leaves and oil are also included in many dishes. Mustard seeds are often fried in oil or ghee to bring out their flavour before being combined with other ingredients. You can substitute the black seeds more commonly found in Western supermarkets.

ONION SEEDS Always used whole in Indian cooking, these tiny black seeds are added to pickles and often sprinkled over the top of naan breads. Onion seeds don't have anything to do with the vegetable, but they look similar to the plant's seed, hence the name.

PAPRIKA Used for colour and flavour, this bright red-orange spice comes from a variety of red pepper. Although similar in colour to chilli powder and cayenne, paprika has a mild flavour and is used in far greater quantities.

PEPPERCORNS These are available in three colours - white (ripe berries), black (unripened berries dried until dark greenish black in colour) and green (unripe berries). The black berries with their warm, aromatic flavour are most frequently used in Indian cooking. Peppercorns are used whole in dishes such as biryani (they are not meant to be eaten and should be left on the side of the plate), or they may be ground, in which case they should be freshly milled as required as they quickly lose their flavour.

POPPY SEEDS In India, poppy seeds are white, not black, and used for their thickening properties. Look for white seeds in Asian grocery stores and some health food stores; do not substitute black poppy seeds as the flavour is very different.

SAFFRON The most expensive of all spices, saffron strands are the stamens of a type of crocus. They give dishes a rich, golden colour, as well as adding a distinctive, slightly bitter taste. Some books recommend substituting turmeric for saffron, but although the colours are similar, the tastes are not. Saffron is sold as a powder or in strands. Saffron strands are more expensive but do have a superior flavour.

TAMARIND Vegetable dishes are often given a sharp, sour flavour with the inclusion of tamarind juice. This is made from the semi-dried, compressed pulp of the tamarind tree. You can buy bars of the pungent-smelling pulp in Asian grocery stores. Store it in a tightly sealed plastic bag or air-tight container.

TURMERIC This aromatic root is dried and ground to produce a distinctive bright yellow-orange powder. It has a warm, aromatic smell and a full, somewhat musty taste.

VARK This is edible silver that is used to decorate elaborate dishes prepared for the most special occasions and celebrations, such as weddings. It is pure silver that has been beaten until it is wafer thin. It comes with a piece of backing paper which is peeled off as the vark is laid on the cooked food. It is extremely delicate and so must be handled with care. You can buy vark in Indian food stores, and remember that because it is pure silver it should be stored in an air-tight bag or box so it doesn't tarnish.

Yogurt

Rich in protein and calcium, yogurt plays an important part in Indian vegetarian cooking, as well as meat dishes. It is used as a marinade, as a creamy flavouring in curries and sauces and as a cooling accompaniment to hot dishes. Thick natural yogurt most closely resembles the yogurt made in many Indian homes.

When cooking with yogurt, take care not to let it overheat and curdle. To prevent this happening, stir in the yogurt a spoonful at a time at the end of cooking, making sure each spoonful is fully incorporated before adding the next. Alternatively, you can blend the yogurt with a little cornflour (cornstarch) or gram flour (½ tsp for every 150 ml/¼ pint/⅔ cup before adding it to the dish.

COOKING EQUIPMENT

Although Indian cooks are masters of delicious, exotic food, their kitchens are not very differently equipped than those found in Western homes. You won't have to make any major investments in specialist equipment to create authentic-tasting meals.

A large, deep pan similar to a wok and several heavy-based saucepans or flameproof casseroles are the most important pieces of equipment, as most Indian cooking is done on top of the stove. In fact, Indians don't use anything that is the equivalent of a Western stove. The traditional Indian oven, called a tandoor, was made of clay and built into the ground, but it is more a feature of restaurant cooking today and very few homes have one. In rural areas, cooking is done on a basic coal- or wood-burning stove built near the floor in the corner of the kitchen. The cook squats in front of the stove or sits on a low stool next to it. Here is a guide to the everyday pieces of equipment needed to produce authentic Indian meals.

Blender

Use a blender to quickly mix cooling drinks, such as the yogurt-based lassi. As an alternative, put all the ingredients in a bowl and use a whisk to blend them.

Degchi

This handleless pan is made of aluminium or brass, has a tight-fitting lid and is similar to the traditional French daubière. Used for cooking slowly braised dishes, its lid is designed to hold hot coals so ingredients are gently cooked by heat from the top as well as the bottom. A heavy-based flameproof casserole will produce similar results.

Food processor

Although not essential, modern Indian cooks find a food processor the most efficient way of coping with all the chopping involved in Indian cooking. It is also useful for chopping large amounts of fresh herbs and making pastes from garlic, ginger and onions. A small food processor, or coffee grinder, is ideal for grinding spices. If you choose this option instead of a pestle and mortar, however, remember to use it exclusively for grinding spices as it will flavour any other foods.

Frying pan (skillet)

A non-stick frying pan (skillet) is useful for dry-frying seeds and spices to bring out their flavours before they are ground.

Karahi

This is an Indian version of the versatile Chinese wok. It is used for deep-frying or for slowly simmering meat, poultry, seafood and pulse dishes. Many Indian homes have two karahis, a deep one with a narrow top which is used for

deep-frying, and a shallower one with a much wider top which is used for occasional stir-frying and simmering. Like a wok it is the curved sides that make this such a useful piece of equipment, because the sides provide a much larger cooking surface than a conventional frying pan (skillet) or saucepan. A traditional Chinese wok is a suitable substitute. Woks come in numerous sizes and are made of various materials, such as cast iron, aluminium, stainless-steel and even brass. You can also buy woks with non-stick finishes, which are particularly useful if you want to reduce the amount of fat in some recipes. When you buy a wok, look for one with one long wooden handle or two wooden handles on the sides so you can grip it without burning your hands. Some woks, especially those made of cast iron, are very heavy, so it is a good idea to pick one up to make sure you can handle it easily. Most woks need a ring that sits over the burner to keep the wok steady while you cook.

Knives

Indian cooking can involve a great deal of chopping, so firm knives with a sharp blade are invaluable. A medium-sized all-purpose knife, called a cook's or kitchen knife, is ideal for most chores, but a flexible, thin-bladed filleting knife is best for filleting fish, and a rigid boning knife is needed for removing meat and poultry bones. Carbon steel can be sharpened very finely, but stainless steel is the usual choice for kitchen knives because it is so easy to take care of. Unlike carbon steel, it doesn't have to be kept dry to prevent it from rusting.

Pestle and mortar

It is easy to buy ground spices and prepared spice mixtures in supermarkets but the flavour of freshly ground spices is vastly superior. A heavy pestle and mortar is useful if you want to grind your own spices. A good quality set will have a slightly rough surface on the interior of the mortar and on the end of the pestle. They may be made from vitrified porcelain, unglazed porcelain, stone, wood, marble or sometimes even heavy-duty glass.

Saucepans

Several medium saucepans with heavy bases are useful for cooking pulses and rice and vegetable dishes. The heavy base is important because it helps to distribute heat evenly, and also retains heat once the pan is taken off the heat. Pans with tight-fitting lids mean they can double as casseroles for cooking on top of the stove, which is useful when you are cooking some of the rice recipes, such pilaus and biryanis. Various materials are used in the manufacture of saucepans and it is a matter of personal choice which you use. Stainless steel is popular because it is hard wearing and easy to clean, but on its own it is not a good conductor of heat. If you want a stainless steel pan, buy one made of heavy-gauge stainless steel or one with copper or aluminium in the base.

Skewers

A supply of stainless steel or bamboo skewers are useful for barbecuing spicy kebabs and some tandoori recipes. Bamboo skewers should be soaked in water for about 30 minutes before use, to prevent them burning. When you buy stainless steel skewers, choose flat, rather than round ones as these hold the ingredients in place when you turn the skewer. If you rub the skewer with vegetable oil before you put any food on it, the cooked food will come off easily.

Tava

This is the traditional flat griddle used for cooking some Indian breads. A large frying pan (skillet) makes an adequate substitute.

Thali

A large rimmed metal plate that comes with several metal bowls, called katoris. Use thalis if you want to serve your Indian meal in the authentic way. Each person has their own thali, with a portion of each dish in each bowl. Made of aluminium or brass (sometimes silver or even gold), you can buy thalis from Asian grocery stores.

Tongs

A pair of long-handled tongs are essential for lifting sizzling food from hot fat when you are deep-frying, or for turning ingredients under a hot grill (broiler).

COOKING TECHNIQUES

The names of Indian cooking techniques are often incorporated into recipe titles on menus. Some of the ones you are most likely to come across are included in the following list.

Barbecuing

Before modern kitchens were installed, much of the cooking in India was done over coal or wood fires, and barbecued food remains a favourite. Tandoori chicken, marinated in yogurt and spices which give its glorious reddish-brown colour, is a popular dish for barbecuing, as are all forms of kebabs.

Bhaghar

This is a simple technique which adds richness and flavour to meat, fish, vegetable, and especially pulse dishes, and counteracts bland flavours. Ghee or vegetable oil is heated in a heavy-based frying pan (skillet), then whole spices and seeds are added and fried until they are golden brown and sizzling. The contents of the pan are poured over the dish a few minutes before serving. The dish is kept covered until ready to serve, to retain all the aromas.

Bharta

This term describes puréed vegetables. Aubergines (eggplant) are often prepared in this way, first being cooked over a charcoal or wood fire so they develop a smoky flavour.

Bhoona

Also known as brown frying, this technique involves stir-frying onions, garlic, ginger and spices until they turn golden brown. Meat and poultry dishes with reddish-brown sauces often begin with this process and it is an important technique in preparing the classic Mogul dishes of northern India. When chopped or sliced onions are prepared this way they are slowly cooked in ghee, or a vegetable oil, until they turn golden, then the spices are stirred in and the stir-frying continues until the onions lose all their moisture and turn a dark, rich brown.

Sukka bhoona in a title indicates that the dish has been sautéed, and this style of dish is usually made with the best, most tender cuts of meat.

Curry

The word 'curry' has become a universal euphemism for Indian cooking and food. Although a dish called a curry does exist, this single word does not do justice to the richly varied dishes and cooking styles of the Indian sub-continent. It is simply a Western way of pronouncing 'kari', a southern Tamil word for sauce or the fragrant leaves of the kari tree. These dried leaves are a main ingredient in a spice mixture called kari podi, which has become known as curry powder. Authentic curries are cooked slowly and never include a marinade, yogurt or cream as in other spicy dishes. Because the cooking process is so slow and gentle, meat curries are usually made with meat from older animals or the tougher cuts. When vegetables such as peas or potatoes are included in a meat curry, they are usually added towards the end of the cooking time.

Do pyaza

A slowly braised dish combining both cooked and raw onions. The main ingredient, usually meat, is gently cooked with half the onions until very tender, then a second batch of raw onions is stirred in towards the end of cooking to give extra texture and taste. Traditional recipes use 900 g/2 lb onions for each 450 g/1 lb meat. You will also see this dish spelled as dopiaza.

Dum

Similar to pot-roasting, this is the Indian method of cooking ingredients in a tightly sealed container on top of the stove. Traditionally, a pan called a degchi is used, set over hot ashes and with hot coals in its lid. A flameproof casserole is a good substitute, as long as it can be tightly sealed. One method of sealing a container is to make a simple flour and water dough, form it into a roll, place it around the rim and press down the lid. Alternatively, put a large piece of foil under the lid and scrunch the over-hanging foil around the sides.

Korma

These are slowly braised dishes, many of which are the rich and spicy, Persian-inspired Mogul dishes served on special occasions. Yogurt is often featured, both as a marinade and as the cooking liquid. In a properly cooked korma, prime tender cuts of meat are used, and the small amount of cooking liquid is absorbed by the meat to produce a deliciously succulent result. A heavy-based cooking container with a tight-fitting lid is essential for a korma.

Marinating

This is a technique widely used to add flavour and tenderize less expensive cuts of meat and seafood before they are baked or grilled (broiled), or cooked in a traditional tandoor oven. Sometimes the ingredients are cut into small pieces and submerged in a marinade, while in other recipes the marinade is brushed on to whole fish or chicken breasts. Heavily spiced yogurt is a popular marinade, especially for ingredients that are cooked over charcoal, under a grill (broiler) or in a tandoor. The yogurt turns into a thin crust as it cooks, protecting the flesh beneath. Lemon and lime juices are also used for marinating, as well as paw-paw (papaya), which has a tenderizing effect.

Talawa

This refers to meat, seafood, poultry or vegetables that are coated in crumbs or a batter and deep-fried until golden on the outside and tender in the centre. You will also see these dishes referred to as talana.

APPETIZERS

Whether you are planning a full-scale dinner party, an informal buffet or a nourishing family meal, don't forget to include a starter or a few appetizers to tease the tastebuds at the beginning of the meal. Starters or hors d'oeuvres are not generally served as such on an Indian menu – all the dishes are served at once, rather than as separate courses. However, as some people may prefer to eat Indian food in a Western way, dishes such as chicken koftas, butterfly prawns or spicy mini kebabs make for a typical beginning. Use hot spices cautiously in such palate-enticing dishes, and serve with a yogurt and cucumber cool dipping sauce. Alternatively, do as the Indians do and serve a selection of snack foods such as bhajis and pakoras before the main meal. These make perfect finger food to serve with drinks.

Many of these dishes would also be ideal for taking on a picnic – a favourite Indian family pastime. A common Sunday activity is to take a picnic to the town maidan or green space, and spend a long lazy afternoon with family and friends chatting, eating and snoozing, and maybe throwing a few cricket balls at a makeshift wicket!

Butterfly Prawns (Shrimp)

*These prawns (shrimp) look stunning when presented on the skewers,
and they will certainly be an impressive prelude to the main meal.*

SERVES 2–4

INGREDIENTS

8 wooden skewers
500 g/1 lb or 16 raw tiger prawns
(shrimp), shelled, leaving tails intact
juice of 2 limes
1 tsp cardamom seeds
2 tsp cumin seeds, ground
2 tsp coriander seeds, ground
½ tsp ground cinnamon
1 tsp ground turmeric
1 garlic clove, crushed
1 tsp cayenne
2 tbsp oil
cucumber slices, to garnish

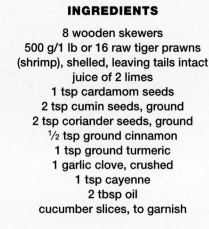

1 Soak 8 wooden skewers in water for 20 minutes. Cut the prawns (shrimp) lengthways in half down to the tail, so that they flatten out to a symmetrical shape.

2 Thread a prawn (shrimp) on to 2 wooden skewers, with the tail between them, so that, when laid flat, the skewers hold the prawn (shrimp) in shape. Thread another 3 prawns (shrimp) on to these 2 skewers in the same way. Repeat until you have 4 sets of 4 prawns (shrimp) each.

3 Lay the skewered prawns (shrimp) in a non-porous, non-metallic dish, and sprinkle over the lime juice.

4 Combine the spices and the oil, and coat the prawns (shrimp) well in the mixture.

5 Cover and chill for 4 hours.

6 Cook over a hot barbecue or in a grill (broiler) pan lined with foil under a preheated grill (broiler) for 6 minutes, turning once.

7 Serve immediately, garnished with cucumber and accompanied by a sweet chutney – Walnut Chutney (page 228) is ideal.

Step *1*

Step *2*

Step *3*

Minted Onion Bhajis

Gram flour (also known as besan flour) is a fine yellow flour made from chick peas and is available from supermarkets and Asian food shops.

MAKES 12

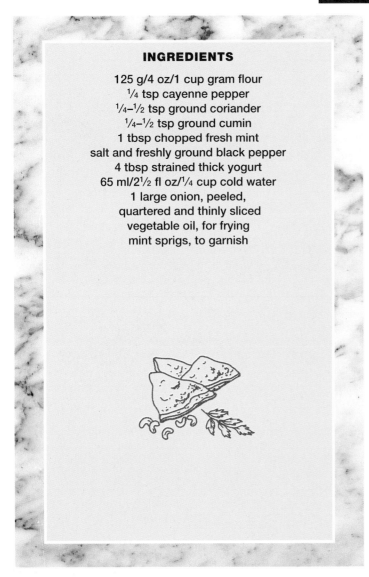

INGREDIENTS

125 g/4 oz/1 cup gram flour
¼ tsp cayenne pepper
¼–½ tsp ground coriander
¼–½ tsp ground cumin
1 tbsp chopped fresh mint
salt and freshly ground black pepper
4 tbsp strained thick yogurt
65 ml/2½ fl oz/¼ cup cold water
1 large onion, peeled,
quartered and thinly sliced
vegetable oil, for frying
mint sprigs, to garnish

1 Put the gram flour into a bowl, add the cayenne pepper, coriander, cumin and mint and season with salt and pepper to taste. Stir in the yogurt, water and sliced onion and mix well together.

2 One-third fill a large, deep frying pan with oil and heat until very hot. Drop heaped spoonfuls of the mixture, a few at a time, into the hot oil and use two forks to neaten the mixture into rough ball-shapes.

3 Fry the bhajis until rich golden brown and cooked through, turning frequently. Drain on absorbent paper towels and keep warm while cooking the remainder in the same way. Serve hot or warm.

Step *1*

Step *2*

Step *3*

Bite-Sized Bajees

*Don't be surprised at the shape these form – they are odd but look lovely
when arranged on a tray with the yogurt dipping sauce.*

MAKES 20

INGREDIENTS

2 heaped tbsp gram flour
½ tsp turmeric
½ tsp cumin seeds, ground
1 tsp garam masala
pinch of cayenne
1 egg
1 large onion, quartered and sliced
1 tbsp chopped fresh coriander (cilantro)
3 tbsp breadcrumbs (optional)
oil for deep-frying
salt

SAUCE

1 tsp coriander seeds, ground
1½ tsp cumin seeds, ground
250 ml/8 fl oz/1 cup natural yogurt
salt and pepper

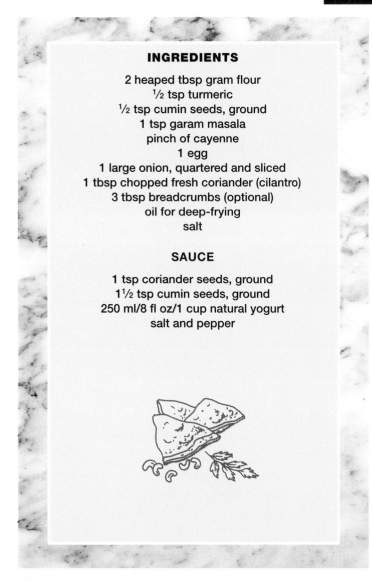

1 Put the gram flour into a large bowl and mix in the spices. Make a well in the centre and add the egg. Stir to form a gluey mixture. Add the onion and sprinkle on a little salt. Add the coriander (cilantro) and stir. If the mixture is not stiff enough, add the breadcrumbs.

2 Heat the oil for deep-frying over a medium heat until fairly hot – it should just be starting to smoke.

3 Push a teaspoonful of the mixture into the oil with a second teaspoon to form fairly round balls. The bajees should firm up quite quickly. Cook in batches of 8–10. Keep stirring them so that they brown evenly. Drain on plenty of paper towels and keep them warm in the oven until ready to serve.

4 To make the sauce, roast the spices in a frying pan (skillet). Remove from the heat and stir in the yogurt. Season well.

Step *1*

Step *3*

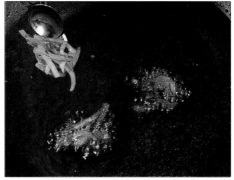

Step *4*

Spicy Bites

Here are three delicious morsels to whet your appetite before a meal. Use
courgettes (zucchini) with the flowers still attached, if you can find them.

SERVES 4

INGREDIENTS

SPICED NUTS

125 g/4 oz/1 cup mixed nuts, such as peanuts,
cashews and blanched almonds
1 dried red chilli
1 tsp sunflower oil
1 garlic clove
½ tsp salt
1 tsp garam masala
½ tsp clear honey

MUSSEL MORSELS

1 kg/2 lb small mussels, scrubbed
3 tbsp mayonnaise
1 tsp garam masala
½ red chilli, seeded and chopped finely
2 spring onions (scallions), chopped finely
45 g/1½ oz/¾ cup white breadcrumbs
salt

DEEP-FRIED COURGETTES (ZUCCHINI)

125 g/4 oz/1 cup plain (all-purpose) flour
½ tsp each turmeric and cayenne
150 ml/¼ pint/⅔ cup water
2 eggs
vegetable oil
1 courgette (zucchini), cut into batons

SPICED NUTS

1 Cook the nuts in a dry, heavy-based pan over a moderate heat until the oil comes off, about 5 minutes. Add the remaining ingredients except the honey, and cook for a further 3 minutes, stirring frequently. Add the honey and cook for 2 minutes.

2 Remove from the heat and turn into a serving dish.

MUSSEL MORSELS

1 Put a little water in the bottom of a large pan. Discard any mussels that are not firmly closed. Add the mussels and cover the pan. Set over a high heat and leave for 5 minutes; do not uncover. Drain the mussels and discard any unopened ones. Remove the shells and reserve.

2 Chop the mussel meat finely. Stir the mayonnaise into the mussel meat. Add the remaining ingredients and season to taste. Spoon the mixture back into the shells, and arrange on a plate.

DEEP-FRIED COURGETTES (ZUCCHINI)

1 Sift the flour and spices together, Add the water, eggs and 1 tablespoon oil. Whisk until smooth.

2 Heat some oil in a wok. Dip the batons into the batter, and drop into the oil. When evenly cooked, remove and drain on paper towels.

Step *1 : Spiced nuts*

Step *1 : Mussel morsels*

Step *2 : Mussel morsels*

Garlicky Mushroom Pakoras

Whole button mushrooms are dunked in a spiced garlicky batter and deep fried until golden.

SERVES 6

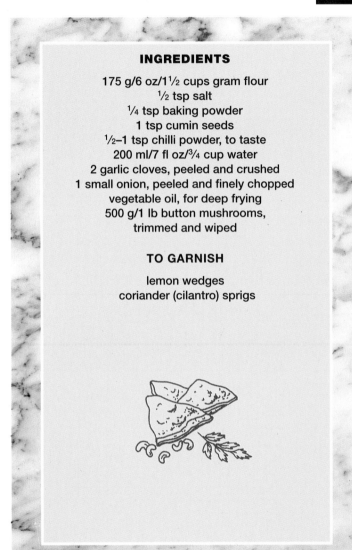

INGREDIENTS

175 g/6 oz/1½ cups gram flour
½ tsp salt
¼ tsp baking powder
1 tsp cumin seeds
½–1 tsp chilli powder, to taste
200 ml/7 fl oz/¾ cup water
2 garlic cloves, peeled and crushed
1 small onion, peeled and finely chopped
vegetable oil, for deep frying
500 g/1 lb button mushrooms,
trimmed and wiped

TO GARNISH

lemon wedges
coriander (cilantro) sprigs

1 Put the gram flour, salt, baking powder, cumin and chilli powder into a bowl and mix well together. Make a well in the centre of the mixture and gradually stir in the water, mixing to form a batter.

2 Stir the crushed garlic and the chopped onion into the batter and leave the mixture to infuse for 10 minutes. One-third fill a deep-fat fryer or pan with vegetable oil and heat to 180°C/350°F or until hot enough to brown a cube of day-old bread in 30 seconds. Lower the basket into the hot oil.

3 Meanwhile, mix the mushrooms into the batter, stirring to coat. Remove a few at a time and place them into the hot oil. Fry for about 2 minutes or until golden brown.

4 Remove from the pan with a slotted spoon and drain on paper towels while cooking the remainder in the same way. Serve hot, sprinkled with coarse salt and garnished with lemon wedges and coriander (cilantro) sprigs.

Step *1*

Step *3*

Step *4*

Pakoras

These vegetable fritters are simple to make and extremely good to eat. They may be served as a tasty starter or as an accompaniment to a main course.

SERVES 4-6

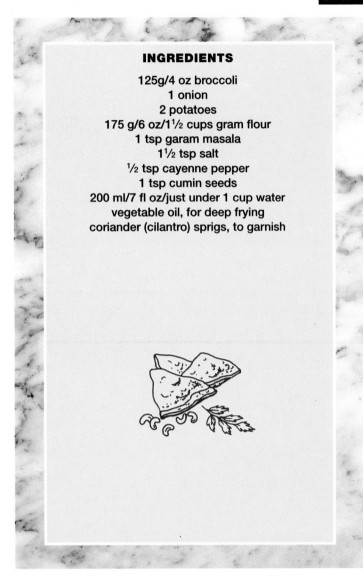

INGREDIENTS

125g/4 oz broccoli
1 onion
2 potatoes
175 g/6 oz/1½ cups gram flour
1 tsp garam masala
1½ tsp salt
½ tsp cayenne pepper
1 tsp cumin seeds
200 ml/7 fl oz/just under 1 cup water
vegetable oil, for deep frying
coriander (cilantro) sprigs, to garnish

1 Cut the broccoli into small florets, discarding most of the stalk and cook in a pan of boiling, salted water for 4 minutes. Drain well, return to the pan and shake dry over a low heat for a few moments. Place the broccoli on absorbent paper towels to completely dry while preparing the other vegetables.

2 Peel and thinly slice the onion and separate into rings. Peel and thinly slice the potatoes and pat dry.

3 Place the gram flour in a bowl with the garam masala, salt, cayenne pepper and cumin seeds. Make a well in the centre, add the water and then mix to form a smooth batter.

4 One-third fill a deep fat fryer or pan with oil and heat to 190°C/375°F or until a cube of day-old bread browns in 30 seconds. Dip the vegetables into the batter to coat, then lower into the hot oil and fry, in batches, for 3–4 minutes or until golden brown and crisp. Drain on absorbent paper towels and keep warm while cooking the remainder in the same way. Serve the pakoras hot, garnished with sprigs of coriander (cilantro).

Step *1*

Step *4*

Step *4*

Vegetable & Cashew Samosas

These delicious little fried pastries are really quite simple to make. Serve them hot as a starter to an Indian meal or cold as a tasty picnic or lunch-box snack.

MAKES 12

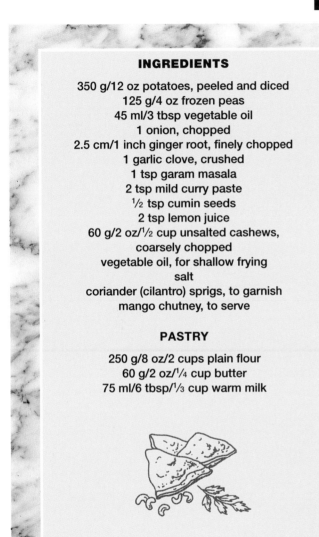

INGREDIENTS

350 g/12 oz potatoes, peeled and diced
125 g/4 oz frozen peas
45 ml/3 tbsp vegetable oil
1 onion, chopped
2.5 cm/1 inch ginger root, finely chopped
1 garlic clove, crushed
1 tsp garam masala
2 tsp mild curry paste
½ tsp cumin seeds
2 tsp lemon juice
60 g/2 oz/½ cup unsalted cashews,
coarsely chopped
vegetable oil, for shallow frying
salt
coriander (cilantro) sprigs, to garnish
mango chutney, to serve

PASTRY

250 g/8 oz/2 cups plain flour
60 g/2 oz/¼ cup butter
75 ml/6 tbsp/⅓ cup warm milk

1 Cook the potatoes in a saucepan of boiling, salted water for 5 minutes. Add the peas and cook for a further 4 minutes or until the potato is tender. Drain well. Heat the oil in a frying pan, add the onion, potato and pea mixture, ginger, garlic and spices and fry for 2 minutes. Stir in the lemon juice and cook gently, uncovered, for 2 minutes. Remove from the heat, slightly mash the potato and peas, then add the cashews, mix well and season with salt.

2 To make the pastry, put the flour in a bowl and rub in the butter finely. Mix in the milk to form a dough. Knead lightly and divide into 6 portions. Form each into a ball and roll out on a lightly floured surface to an 18 cm/7 inch round. Cut each one in half.

3 Divide the filling equally between each semi-circle of pastry, spreading it out to within 5 mm/¼ inch of the edges. Brush the edges of pastry all the way round with water and fold over to form triangular shapes, sealing the edges well together to enclose the filling completely.

4 One-third fill a large, deep frying pan with oil and heat to 180°C/350°F or until hot enough to brown a cube of bread in 30 seconds. Fry the samosas, a few at a time, turning frequently until golden brown and heated through. Drain on paper towels and keep warm while cooking the remainder in the same way. Garnish with sprigs of coriander (cilantro) and serve hot.

Step *2*

Step *3*

Step *4*

Spiced Chicken Koftas with Lime Pickle

Koftas are spicy meat balls. In this recipe they are made with chicken, but you could use lamb or beef. Lime pickle is available in Asian food stores and some supermarkets.

SERVES 4

INGREDIENTS

500 g/1lb skinned and boned chicken,
chopped coarsely
1 garlic clove
2.5 cm/1 inch piece ginger root, grated
4 tsp garam masala
½ tsp ground turmeric
2 tbsp chopped fresh coriander (cilantro)
½ green (bell) pepper, chopped coarsely
2 fresh green chillies, seeded
½ tsp salt
6 tbsp oil
1 jar lime pickle, to serve
lime wedges, to garnish

1 Put all the ingredients except the oil and lime pickle into a food processor or blender and process until the mixture is chopped finely. Alternatively, finely chop the chicken, garlic, ginger, (bell) pepper and chillies, and mix together in a bowl with the garam masala, turmeric, coriander (cilantro) and salt.

2 Shape the mixture into 16 small balls.

3 Heat the oil in a karahi or wok and fry the koftas for 8–10 minutes, turning them occasionally to ensure they cook evenly. If you cannot fit all the koftas into the pan at once, keep the first batch warm in a low oven, while you fry the remaining koftas.

4 Drain the koftas on paper towels and serve hot with lime pickle.

Step *1*

Step *2*

Step *3*

Rashmi Kebabs

This is a variation on Sheek Kebab. A little attention is needed when making the egg 'nets', but the extra effort is worth it, as the effect is very impressive.

SERVES 4

INGREDIENTS

1 red (bell) pepper, seeded
and chopped coarsely
1 tsp chilli powder
2 tsp coriander seeds
2 tsp cumin seeds
½ tsp salt
2 cloves garlic
½ tsp pepper
500 g/1 lb/2 cups minced (ground) lamb
4 eggs
oil for deep frying

1 Grind the red (bell) pepper, chilli powder, coriander seeds, cumin seeds, salt, garlic and black pepper in a food processor or blender. Alternatively, grind the coriander and cumin in a pestle and mortar, chop the red (bell) pepper and garlic very finely and mix with the ground spices, salt, chilli powder and black pepper.

2 Transfer the spice mixture to a bowl and add the lamb and 1 of the eggs. Mix well to evenly distribute the egg and bind the mixture together.

3 Divide the lamb mixture into 8. Shape 1 piece into a ball. Put the ball on a clean plate and gently squash the top with the palm of your hand, to form a patty. Repeat with the remaining pieces. If possible, refrigerate the kebabs for at least 30 minutes.

4 Cook the kebabs under a preheated hot grill (broiler) for 15 minutes, turning once.

5 Meanwhile, make the egg nets. Beat together the remaining eggs. Fill a large frying pan (skillet) with oil to a depth of 5–7.5 cm/2–3 inches. Heat until a cube of bread that is dropped in sizzles in 1 minute.

6 Trickle the egg off the end of a spoon into the oil, crisscrossing the lines in a grid shape. It will take only seconds to cook. Remove and drain on plenty of paper towels. Repeat until all the egg is used. Wrap each kebab in 1–2 egg nets. Serve warm.

Step *1*

Step *2*

Step *6*

Lamb & Tomato Koftas

These little meatballs, served with a minty yogurt dressing, can be prepared well in advance, ready to cook when required.

SERVES 4

INGREDIENTS

250 g/8 oz/1 cup finely minced (ground) lean lamb
1½ onions
1–2 garlic cloves, crushed
1 dried red chilli, finely chopped (optional)
2–3 tsp garam masala
2 tbsp chopped fresh mint
2 tsp lemon juice
2 tbsp vegetable oil
4 small tomatoes, quartered
mint sprigs, to garnish
salt

YOGURT DRESSING

150 ml/¼ pint/⅔ cup strained thick yogurt
5 cm/2 inch piece cucumber, grated
2 tbsp chopped fresh mint
½ tsp toasted cumin seeds (optional)

1 Place the minced lamb in a bowl. Finely chop 1 onion and add to the bowl with the garlic and chilli, if using. Stir in the garam masala, mint and lemon juice and season well with salt. Mix the ingredients well together.

2 Divide the mixture in half, then divide each half into 10 equal portions and form each into a small ball. Roll balls in the oil to coat. Quarter the remaining onion half and separate into layers.

3 Thread 5 of the balls, 4 tomato quarters and some of the onion layers on to each of 4 bamboo or metal skewers. Brush the vegetables with the remaining oil and cook under a hot grill for about 10 minutes, turning frequently until they are browned all over and cooked through.

4 Meanwhile, prepare the yogurt dressing. Mix the yogurt with the cucumber, mint and toasted cumin seeds, if using. Garnish the lamb koftas with mint sprigs and serve hot with the yogurt dressing.

Step *1*

Step *2*

Step *3*

Sheek Kebabs

*Sheek Kebabs are delicious cooked over a barbecue. Serve in pitta bread
for great party food. The cooked meat can also be chopped into a salad.*

SERVES 4–8

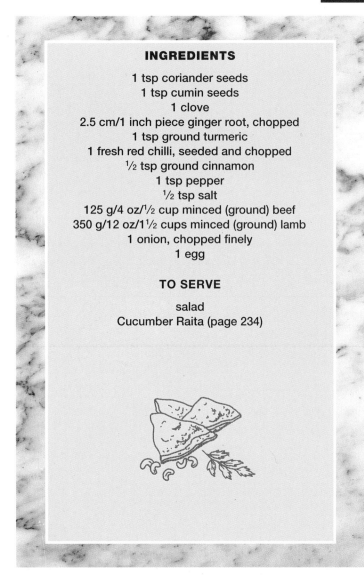

INGREDIENTS

1 tsp coriander seeds
1 tsp cumin seeds
1 clove
2.5 cm/1 inch piece ginger root, chopped
1 tsp ground turmeric
1 fresh red chilli, seeded and chopped
½ tsp ground cinnamon
1 tsp pepper
½ tsp salt
125 g/4 oz/½ cup minced (ground) beef
350 g/12 oz/1½ cups minced (ground) lamb
1 onion, chopped finely
1 egg

TO SERVE

salad
Cucumber Raita (page 234)

1 Grind together the coriander, cumin, clove and ginger in a pestle and mortar. Mix in the turmeric, chilli, cinnamon, pepper and salt.

2 Combine the spice mixture with the beef, lamb and onion.

3 Make a well in the centre of the meat mixture, add the egg and mix in thoroughly.

4 Press one-eighth of the meat mixture around an oiled skewer, to form a shape about 10 cm/4 inches long and 2.5 cm/1 inch thick. Repeat with the remaining meat mixture.

5 If possible, leave to rest in the refrigerator for at least 1 hour.

6 Cook the kebabs under a preheated medium grill (broiler) for about 20 minutes, turning once or twice, until the meat juices run clear when the thickest part of the meat balls is pierced with the point of a sharp knife.

7 Serve with salad and cucumber raita.

Step *1*

Step *3*

Step *4*

Masala Kebabs

Indian kebab dishes are not necessarily cooked on a skewer; they can also be served in a dish and are always dry dishes with no sauce.

SERVES 4-6

INGREDIENTS

1 dried bay leaf
2.5 cm/1 inch piece ginger root, chopped
2.5 cm/1 inch cinnamon stick
1 tsp coriander seeds
½ tsp salt
1 tsp fennel seeds
1 tsp chilli powder
1 tsp garam masala
1 tsp lemon juice
1 tsp ground turmeric
1 tbsp oil
750 g/1½ lb lamb neck fillet

TO GARNISH

fresh coriander (cilantro) sprigs
lemon wedges

TO SERVE:

bread
chutney

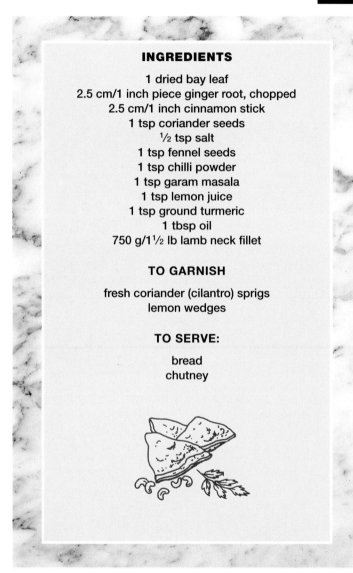

1 Use a food processor, blender or pestle and mortar to grind together the bay leaf, ginger, cinnamon, coriander seeds, salt, fennel seeds and chilli powder.

2 Combine this spice mix with the garam masala, lemon juice, turmeric and oil in a large bowl.

3 Cut the lamb into 5mm/¼ inch slices.

4 Add to the spice mix and leave to marinate at room temperature for about 1 hour, or in the refrigerator for 3 hours or overnight.

5 Spread out the pieces of lamb on a baking sheet and cook in a preheated oven, 200°C/400°F/Gas Mark 6, for 20 minutes until well done. Transfer to paper towels to drain any excess fat.

6 Thread 3 or 4 pieces of meat on to each skewer and garnish with fresh coriander (cilantro) sprigs and lemon wedges. Serve hot with bread and chutney.

Step *1*

Step *3*

Step *5*

FISH DISHES

*At first glance India may not be considered a great
fish-eating nation, but it has a coastline stretching for
over 4000 km (2500 miles), and with internal waters
can supply over 2000 varieties of fish!
Fish is very popular in some areas and plays
an important part in the diet. There is a vast array
of fresh seafood in southern India, Bengal, Calcutta and
its environs, and as far north as Darjeeling. North
of Calcutta, rivers and streams flow from the
Himalayas. The water is very clean and pure,
and a great variety of river fish is caught. Lake fish
are also enjoyed when available.
Many fish and shellfish are simply grilled, whole or on
skewers, after sprinkling with a few spices and brushing
with mustard oil. Others are fried whole or as fish and
vegetable fritters. Fish with a firm, meaty
texture, like cod, are curried in aromatic sauces and
frequently flavoured with coconut. Countless others
are baked, steamed, poached or roasted with that
characteristic Indian flavour that is based on a masala
of spices that enhances, but does not overwhelm, the
delicate flavour of the fish.*

Indian Grilled Trout

Here is a deliciously simple way of preparing and cooking trout.
It is also good with nice fresh, plump mackerel.

SERVES 4

INGREDIENTS

4 trout, about 250 g/8 oz
6 tbsp ghee or melted butter
1–2 garlic cloves, crushed
1 fresh green chilli, seeded and chopped,
or 1 tsp minced chilli (from a jar)
2.5 cm/1 inch ginger root,
peeled and chopped finely
1½ tsp cumin seeds
1 tsp garam masala
1 tsp ground cumin
finely grated rind of 1 lemon
juice of 2 lemons
salt

TO GARNISH

coriander (cilantro) sprigs
lemon wedges

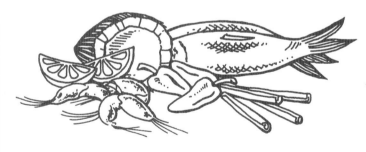

1 Using a sharp knife, carefully make 3 diagonal slashes (not too deep) on each side of the trout. Season the trout and place in a lightly greased grill (broiler) pan.

2 Heat the ghee or butter in a small pan over a low heat, add the crushed garlic, chilli, chopped ginger and spices and cook very gently for 30 seconds, stirring.

3 Remove the pan from the heat and stir the lemon rind and juice into the mixture.

4 Spoon half the mixture over the trout and cook under a moderately hot grill (broiler) for 5–8 minutes or until cooked on one side. Turn the fish over and spoon the remaining mixture over the fish and grill (broil) for a further 5–8 minutes, basting frequently with the juices in pan during cooking.

5 Arrange the trout on a hot serving plate, spoon the pan juices over the fish and garnish with coriander (cilantro) sprigs and lemon wedges. Serve hot.

Step *1*

Step *3*

Step *4*

Indian Cod with Tomatoes

Quick and easy – cod steaks are cooked in a rich tomato and coconut sauce to produce tender, succulent results.

SERVES 4

INGREDIENTS

3 tbsp vegetable oil
4 cod steaks, about 2.5 cm/1 inch thick
1 onion, chopped finely
2 garlic cloves, crushed
1 red (bell) pepper, seeded and chopped
1 tsp ground coriander
1 tsp ground cumin
1 tsp ground turmeric
½ tsp garam masala
425 g/14 oz can chopped tomatoes
150 ml/¼ pint/⅔ cup coconut milk
1–2 tbsp chopped fresh coriander (cilantro)
or parsley
salt and pepper

1 Heat the oil in a frying pan, add the fish steaks, season with salt and pepper and fry until browned on both sides (but not cooked through). Remove from the pan and reserve.

2 Add the onion, garlic, red (bell) pepper and spices and cook very gently for 2 minutes, stirring frequently. Add the tomatoes, bring to the boil and simmer for 5 minutes.

3 Add the fish steaks to the pan and simmer gently for 8 minutes or until the fish is cooked through. Remove from the pan and keep warm on a serving dish.

4 Add the coconut milk and coriander (cilantro) to the pan and reheat gently. Spoon the sauce over the cod steaks and serve immediately.

Step *2*

Step *3*

Step *4*

Masala Fried Fish

*Frying fish is classically Indian, although it does not always spring to
mind when thinking of Indian food.*

SERVES 4–8

INGREDIENTS

8 plaice or other white fish fillets,
about 125–150 g/4–5 oz each
1 tbsp ground turmeric
2 tbsp plain (all-purpose) flour
salt
½ tsp black peppercorns, ground
1 tsp chilli powder
1 tbsp coriander seeds, ground
1 garlic clove, crushed
2 tsp garam masala
oil for deep frying

TO GARNISH

chilli powder
lemon wedges

1 To skin the fish fillets, lay the fillet skin side down with the tail nearest you. Hold the tail end between your thumb and forefinger. Hold a sharp knife at a shallow angle to the fish in your other hand. Holding the fish firmly, make an angled cut between the flesh and the skin, then continue to cut the flesh away from the skin until it is free.

2 In a shallow dish, combine the turmeric, flour, salt, peppercorns, chilli powder, coriander seeds, garlic and garam masala. Mix well.

3 Fill a shallow saucepan or a deep frying pan (skillet) with oil to a depth of 5–7 cm/2–3 inches, and heat to 180° C/350° F.

4 Coat the fish fillets in the spice mix either by shaking gently in a paper bag or turning over in the dish of spice mix until well coated.

5 Deep fry the fish fillets for about 3–5 minutes, turning often until the fish flakes with a fork. Drain on plenty of paper towels.

6 Serve sprinkled with chilli powder, garnished with lemon wedges, and accompanied by a selection of pickles and chutneys.

Step *1*

Step *2*

Step *5*

Spicy Fish & Potato Fritters

You need nice, floury-textured old (main crop) potatoes for making these tasty fritters. Any white fish of your choice may be used.

SERVES 4

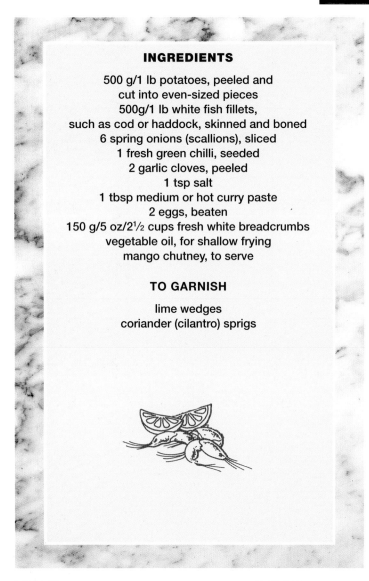

INGREDIENTS

500 g/1 lb potatoes, peeled and
cut into even-sized pieces
500g/1 lb white fish fillets,
such as cod or haddock, skinned and boned
6 spring onions (scallions), sliced
1 fresh green chilli, seeded
2 garlic cloves, peeled
1 tsp salt
1 tbsp medium or hot curry paste
2 eggs, beaten
150 g/5 oz/2½ cups fresh white breadcrumbs
vegetable oil, for shallow frying
mango chutney, to serve

TO GARNISH

lime wedges
coriander (cilantro) sprigs

1 Cook the potatoes in a pan of boiling, salted water until tender. Drain well, return the potatoes to the pan and place over a moderate heat for a few moments to dry off. Cool slightly, then place in a food processor with the fish, onions, chilli, garlic, salt and curry paste. Process until the ingredients are very finely chopped and blended.

2 Turn the potato mixture into a bowl and mix in 2 tablespoons of beaten egg and 60 g/2 oz/1 cup of breadcrumbs. Place the remaining beaten egg and breadcrumbs in separate dishes.

3 Divide the fish mixture into 8 and, using a spoon to help you (the mixture is quite soft), dip first in the beaten egg and then coat in the breadcrumbs, and carefully shape the mixture into ovals.

4 Heat enough oil in a large frying pan for shallow frying and fry the fritters over moderate heat for 3-4 minutes, turning frequently, until golden brown and cooked through. Drain on absorbent paper towels and garnish with lime wedges and coriander (cilantro) sprigs. Serve hot, with mango chutney.

Step *2*

Step *3*

Step *4*

Deep-Fried Battered Fish

The crispy, spicy battered fish is complemented by a tangy fenugreek
dip. The dish makes a delicious and light start to a meal.

SERVES 4

INGREDIENTS

125 g/4 oz/1 cup gram flour or
plain (all-purpose) flour
2 tsp garam masala
4 tsp brown mustard seeds
2 eggs
1 tbsp oil
120–150 ml/4–5 fl oz/½–⅔ cup coconut milk
500 g/1 lb plaice fillets, skinned,
and cut into 1.5 cm/½ inch strips
300 ml/½ pint/1¼ cups oil for deep-frying
lemon wedges, to serve

DIP

150 ml/¼ pint/⅔ cup thick yogurt
2 tbsp chopped fresh fenugreek
½ tsp garam masala
1 tsp tomato purée (paste)

1 Sift the flour into a bowl and add the garam masala and mustard seeds. Make a well in the centre and gradually add the eggs, 1 tablespoon of oil and enough coconut milk to make a batter which has the consistency of thick cream.

2 Coat the fish in the batter and set aside.

3 To make the dip, put the yogurt, fenugreek, garam masala and tomato purée (paste) into a bowl and mix together.

4 Heat the oil in a karahi or wok. Add the fish in batches so the pan is not crowded, and deep-fry for 3–4 minutes until golden brown. Transfer the fish to paper towels to drain then keep warm in a low oven while you cook the rest of the fish.

5 Serve the fish hot with lemon wedges and the dip.

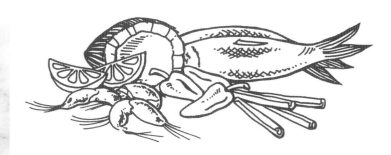

Step *1*

Step *3*

Step *4*

Green Fish Curry

This dish is from southern India. It has a wonderful fresh, hot, exotic taste resulting from the generous amount of fresh herbs, sharp fresh chillies and coconut milk.

SERVES 4

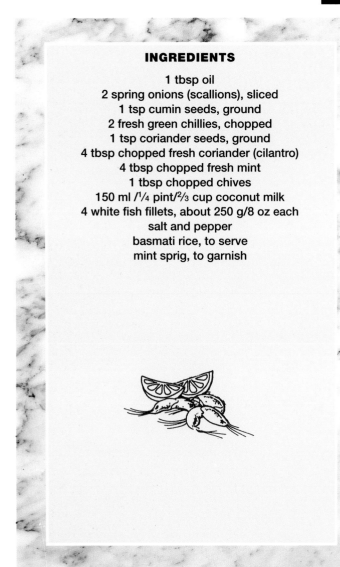

INGREDIENTS

1 tbsp oil
2 spring onions (scallions), sliced
1 tsp cumin seeds, ground
2 fresh green chillies, chopped
1 tsp coriander seeds, ground
4 tbsp chopped fresh coriander (cilantro)
4 tbsp chopped fresh mint
1 tbsp chopped chives
150 ml /¼ pint/⅔ cup coconut milk
4 white fish fillets, about 250 g/8 oz each
salt and pepper
basmati rice, to serve
mint sprig, to garnish

1 Heat the oil in a large frying pan (skillet) or shallow saucepan and add the spring onions (scallions).

2 Stir-fry the spring onions (scallions) over a medium heat until they are softened but not coloured. Stir in the cumin, chillies and ground coriander, and cook them until fragrant.

3 Add the fresh coriander (cilantro), mint, chives and coconut milk and season liberally.

4 Carefully place the fish in the pan and poach for 10–15 minutes until the flesh flakes when tested with a fork.

5 Serve the fish fillets in the sauce with basmati rice and garnish with a mint sprig.

Step *2*

Step *3*

Step *4*

Shrimp Curry & Fruit Sauce

Serve this lightly-spiced dish as part of a buffet meal, or as a refreshingly different lunch dish, with rice or poppadoms.

SERVES 4

INGREDIENTS

2 tbsp vegetable oil
30 g/1 oz/2 tbsp butter
2 onions, chopped finely
2 garlic cloves, chopped finely
1 tsp cumin seeds, lightly crushed
1 tsp ground turmeric
1 tsp paprika
½ tsp chilli powder, or to taste
½ cucumber, diced thinly
60 g/2 oz creamed coconut
425 g/14 oz can chopped tomatoes
1 tbsp tomato purée (paste)
500 g/1 lb frozen shrimps, defrosted
150 ml/¼ pint/⅔ cup thick yogurt
salt

TO GARNISH

2 hard-boiled eggs, quartered
coriander (cilantro) sprigs
onion rings

FRUIT SAUCE

300 ml/½ pint/1¼ cups natural yogurt
¼ tsp salt
1 garlic clove, crushed
2 tbsp fresh mint, chopped
4 tbsp seedless raisins
1 small pomegranate
mint sprig

1 Heat the oil and butter in a frying pan. Add the chopped onions and fry until translucent. Add the garlic and fry for a further minute, until softened but not browned.

2 Stir in the cumin seeds, turmeric, paprika and chilli powder and cook for 2 minutes, stirring. Stir in the creamed coconut, chopped tomatoes and tomato purée (paste) and bring to the boil. Simmer for 10 minutes, or until the sauce has thickened slightly. It should not be at all runny.

3 Remove the pan from the heat and set aside to cool. Stir in the shrimps, cucumber and yogurt. Taste the sauce and adjust the seasoning if necessary. Cover and chill until ready to serve.

4 To make the fruit sauce, place the yogurt in a bowl and stir in the salt, garlic, mint and raisins. Cut the pomegranate in half, scoop out the seeds and discard the white membrane. Stir the seeds into the yogurt, reserving a few for garnish.

5 Transfer the curry to a serving dish and arrange the hard-boiled egg, coriander (cilantro) and onion rings on top. Serve the sauce separately, sprinkled with the reserved pomegranate seeds and mint sprig.

Step *1*

Step *2*

Step *3*

Curried Crab

*Shellfish is a major part of the diet in coastal areas of India. It is frozen
and shipped to all parts India, to be used in a wide variety of dishes.*

SERVES 4

INGREDIENTS

2 tbsp mustard oil
1 tbsp ghee
1 onion, chopped finely
5 cm/2 inch piece ginger root, grated
2 garlic cloves, peeled but left whole
1 tsp ground turmeric
1 tsp salt
1 tsp chilli powder
2 fresh green chillies, chopped
1 tsp paprika
125 g/4 oz/½ cup brown crab meat
350 g/12 oz/1½ cups white crab meat
250 ml/8 fl oz /1 cup natural yogurt
1 tsp garam masala
basmati rice, to serve
fresh coriander (cilantro), to garnish

1 Heat the mustard oil in a large, preferably non-stick, frying pan (skillet), wok or saucepan. When it starts to smoke add the ghee and onion. Stir for 3 minutes over a medium heat until the onion is soft.

2 Stir in the ginger and whole garlic cloves.

3 Add the turmeric, salt, chilli powder, chillies and paprika. Mix thoroughly.

4 Increase the heat and add the crab meat and yogurt. Simmer, stirring occasionally, for 10 minutes until the sauce is thickened slightly. Add garam masala to taste.

5 Serve hot, over plain basmati rice, with the fresh coriander (cilantro) either chopped or in sprigs.

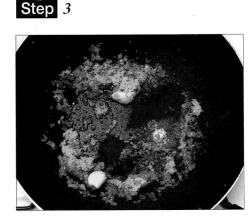

Step *1*

Step *2*

Step *3*

Prawns (Shrimp) & Chilli Sauce

Quick and easy to prepare and extremely good to eat. Use the large and succulent tiger prawns (shrimp) for special occasions.

SERVES 4

INGREDIENTS

4 tbsp ghee or vegetable oil
1 onion, quartered and sliced
1 bunch spring onions (scallions),
trimmed and sliced
1 garlic clove, crushed
1–2 fresh green chillies,
seeded and finely chopped
2.5 cm/1 inch piece ginger root,
finely chopped
1 tsp ground turmeric
1 tsp ground cumin
1 tsp ground coriander
1½ tsp curry powder or paste
425 g/14 oz can chopped tomatoes
150 ml/¼ pint/⅔ cup water
150 ml/¼ pint/⅔ cup double (heavy) cream
500 g/1 lb peeled prawns (shrimp)
1–2 tbsp chopped fresh coriander (cilantro)
salt
coriander (cilantro) sprigs, to garnish

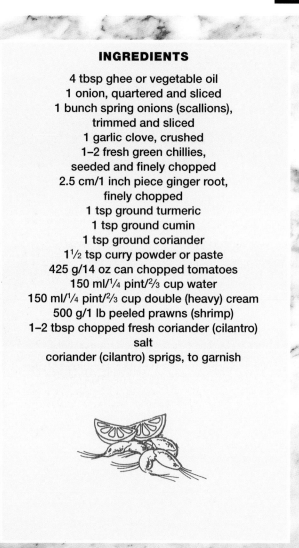

1 Heat the ghee or vegetable oil in a saucepan and fry the onions, garlic and chilli over gentle heat for 3 minutes. Stir in the ginger, spices and curry powder or paste and cook very gently for a further 1 minute, stirring all the time.

2 Stir in the tomatoes and water and bring to the boil, stirring. Reduce the heat and simmer for 10 minutes, stirring occasionally.

3 Add the cream, mix well and simmer for 5 minutes, then add the prawns (shrimp) and coriander (cilantro) and season with salt to taste. Cook gently for 2–3 minutes. Taste and adjust the seasoning, if necessary. Serve garnished with coriander (cilantro) sprigs.

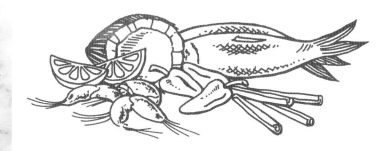

Step *1*

Step *2*

Step *3*

Balti King Prawns (Jumbo Shrimp)

Although prawns (shrimp) are not a traditional ingredient of Balti cooking, they work well with Balti spices and Balti cooking methods.

SERVES 4

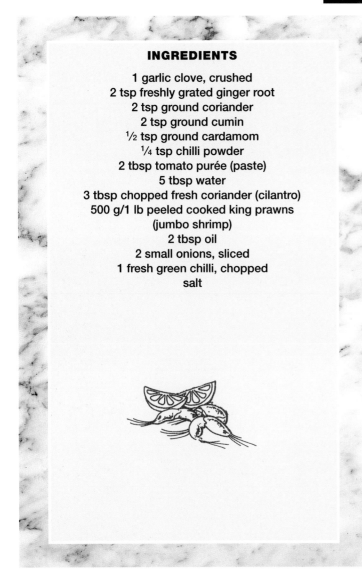

INGREDIENTS

1 garlic clove, crushed
2 tsp freshly grated ginger root
2 tsp ground coriander
2 tsp ground cumin
½ tsp ground cardamom
¼ tsp chilli powder
2 tbsp tomato purée (paste)
5 tbsp water
3 tbsp chopped fresh coriander (cilantro)
500 g/1 lb peeled cooked king prawns (jumbo shrimp)
2 tbsp oil
2 small onions, sliced
1 fresh green chilli, chopped
salt

1 Put the garlic, ginger, ground coriander, cumin, cardamom, chilli powder, tomato purée (paste), 4 tablespoons of the water and 2 tablespoons of the fresh coriander (cilantro) into a bowl. Mix all the ingredients together.

2 Add the prawns (shrimp) to the bowl and leave to marinate for 2 hours.

3 Heat the oil in a karahi or wok, add the onions and stir-fry until golden brown.

4 Add the prawns (shrimp), marinade and the chilli and stir-fry over a medium heat for 5 minutes. Add salt, and the remaining tablespoon of water if the mixture is very dry. Stir-fry over a medium heat for a further 5 minutes.

5 Serve immediately with the remaining fresh chopped coriander (cilantro).

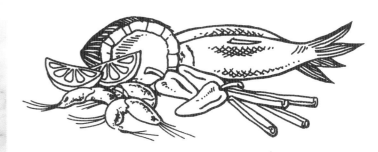

Step *1*

Step *3*

Step *4*

Prawn (Shrimp) Dansak

The lentil purée sauce in this recipe is of Parsi origin and is popular throughout the whole of India.

SERVES 4–6

INGREDIENTS

750 g/1½ lb uncooked tiger prawns
(shrimp) in their shells or 650 g/1 lb 5 oz
peeled tiger prawns (shrimp), cooked
tsp salt
1 bay leaf
3 garlic cloves
90 g/3 oz/⅓ cup split yellow peas,
soaked for 1 hour in cold water and drained
60 g/2 oz/¼ cup red lentils
1 carrot, chopped
1 potato, cut into large dice
3 tbsp drained canned sweetcorn
3 tbsp oil
2 onions, chopped
½ tsp yellow mustard seeds
1½ tsp coriander seeds, ground
½ tsp cumin seeds, ground
½ tsp fenugreek seeds, ground
1½ tsp ground turmeric
1 dried red chilli
425 g/14 oz can tomatoes
½ tsp garam masala
3 tbsp chopped fresh coriander (cilantro)
2 tbsp chopped fresh mint

1 Reserve a few of the prawns (shrimp) for garnish and peel the rest. Set aside. Cook those for the garnish in boiling water for 3–5 minutes if not already cooked.

2 Fill a large saucepan with water and add the salt, bay leaf, 1 garlic clove and the split yellow peas. Bring to the boil and cook for 15 minutes. Add the red lentils, carrot and potato and cook, uncovered, for a further 15 minutes. Drain, discarding the garlic and bay leaf.

3 Purée the cooked vegetables with the sweetcorn in a blender or food processor. Alternatively, use a potato masher to break down the lumps.

4 Crush the remaining garlic. Heat the oil in a large saucepan and cook the onion and garlic for 3–4 minutes. Add the mustard seeds and when they start to pop, stir in the coriander, cumin and fenugreek seeds, turmeric and chilli. Add the prawns (shrimp) and stir over a high heat for 1–2 minutes.

5 Add the tomatoes and the puréed vegetables, and gently simmer. Cook, uncovered, for 30–40 minutes. Stir in the garam masala and taste for seasoning.

6 Serve, sprinkled with the fresh coriander (cilantro) and mint, and garnished with reserved prawns (shrimp).

Step *1*

Step *3*

Step *4*

Prawn (Shrimp) Bhuna

This is a fiery recipe with subtle undertones. As the flavour of the prawns should be noticeable, the spices should not take over this dish.

SERVES 4–6

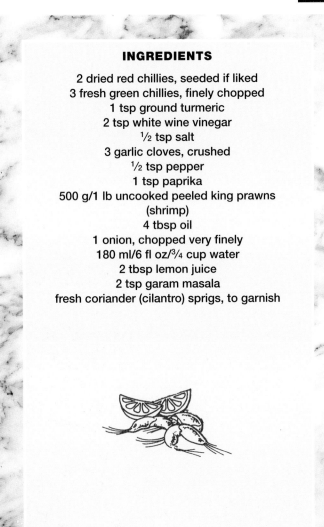

INGREDIENTS

2 dried red chillies, seeded if liked
3 fresh green chillies, finely chopped
1 tsp ground turmeric
2 tsp white wine vinegar
½ tsp salt
3 garlic cloves, crushed
½ tsp pepper
1 tsp paprika
500 g/1 lb uncooked peeled king prawns
(shrimp)
4 tbsp oil
1 onion, chopped very finely
180 ml/6 fl oz/¾ cup water
2 tbsp lemon juice
2 tsp garam masala
fresh coriander (cilantro) sprigs, to garnish

1 Combine the chillies, turmeric, vinegar, salt, garlic, pepper and paprika in a non-metallic bowl. Stir in the prawns and set aside for 10 minutes.

2 Heat the oil in a large frying pan (skillet) or wok, add the onion and fry for 3–4 minutes until soft.

3 Add the prawns (shrimp) and the contents of the bowl to the pan and stir-fry over a high heat for 2 minutes.

4 Reduce the heat, add the water and boil for 10 minutes, stirring occasionally, until the water is evaporated and the curry is fragrant.

5 Stir in the lemon juice and garam masala.

6 Serve garnished with fresh coriander (cilantro) sprigs.

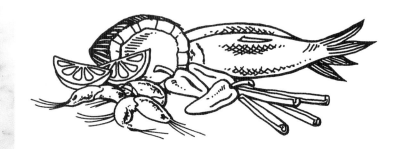

Step *1*

Step *3*

Step *4*

POULTRY DISHES

*Chicken is probably one of the most frequently used
meats in Indian cooking, particularly in northern India
where milder dishes are a speciality and dairy products
more prevalent. The delicate flavour and texture
of chicken combines well with richly flavoured aromatic
sauces based on yogurt, cream and ground nuts which
bring to mind the opulent days of the maharajahs and
nazirs of long-ago India. These sauces have a subtle
balance of flavours and spice mixes, and extra chilli
should not be added to heat them up.
As it does not take long to cook, chicken lends itself well
to the quick stir-fry cooking method, or it
can be quickly roasted tandoori-style. You can either
buy whole chickens and joint them yourself, or buy
chicken pieces, or, for convenience, use boneless chicken
breasts. As in many Asian countries, the chickens used in
India are often free-range and scrawny, but they have a
flavour far superior to our battery-raised birds.
Marinating the chicken for as long as possible really
helps to give it a more interesting flavour.*

Tandoori Chicken

To replicate the intense heat of a traditional tandoor oven, cook the tandoori chicken at a very high temperature, preferably on a barbecue.

SERVES 4

INGREDIENTS

8 small chicken pieces, skinned
3 dried red chillies
1 tsp salt
2 tsp coriander seeds
2 tbsp lime juice
2 garlic cloves, crushed
2.5 cm/1 inch piece ginger root, grated
1 clove
2 tsp garam masala
2 tsp chilli powder
½ onion, chopped
300 ml/½ pint/1¼ cups natural yogurt
1 tbsp chopped fresh coriander (cilantro)
lemon slices, to garnish
Cucumber Raita (page 234), to serve

1 Make 2–3 slashes with a sharp knife in the flesh of the chicken pieces.

2 Crush together the chillies, salt, coriander seeds, lime juice, garlic, ginger and clove. Stir in the garam masala and chilli powder. Transfer to a small saucepan and heat gently until aromatic.

3 Add the onion and fry. Then stir in yogurt and remove pan from heat.

4 Arrange the chicken in a non-metallic dish and pour over the yogurt mixture. Cover and put in the refrigerator to marinate for 4 hours or overnight.

5 Arrange the chicken on a grill (broiler) tray and cook under a preheated very hot grill (broiler) or over a barbecue for 20–30 minutes, turning once, until the chicken juices run clear when the thickest parts of the portions are pierced with a sharp knife.

6 Sprinkle the chicken with chopped fresh coriander (cilantro). Serve hot or cold, garnished with the lemon slices and accompanied by cucumber raita.

Step *2*

Step *3*

Step *4*

Chicken Jalfrezi

This is a quick and tasty way to use leftover roast chicken. The sauce can also be used for any cooked poultry, lamb or beef.

SERVES 4

INGREDIENTS

1 tsp mustard oil
3 tbsp vegetable oil
1 large onion, chopped finely
3 garlic cloves, crushed
1 tbsp tomato purée (paste)
2 tomatoes, peeled and chopped
1 tsp ground turmeric
½ tsp cumin seeds, ground
½ tsp coriander seeds, ground
½ tsp chilli powder
½ tsp garam masala
1 tsp red wine vinegar
1 small red (bell) pepper, chopped
125 g/4 oz/1 cup frozen broad
(fava) beans
500 g/1 lb cooked chicken,
cut into bite-sized pieces
salt
fresh coriander (cilantro) sprigs, to garnish

1 Heat the mustard oil in a large, frying pan (skillet) set over a high heat for about 1 minute until it begins to smoke. Add the vegetable oil, reduce the heat and then add the onion and the garlic. Fry oil, garlic and onion until they are golden.

2 Add the tomato purée (paste), chopped tomatoes, turmeric, ground cumin and coriander seeds, chilli powder, garam masala and vinegar to the frying pan (skillet). Stir the mixture until fragrant.

3 Add the red (bell) pepper and broad (fava) beans and stir for 2 minutes until the pepper is softened.Stir in the chicken, and salt to taste. Simmer gently for 6–8 minutes until the chicken is heated through and the beans are tender.

4 Serve garnished with coriander (cilantro) sprigs.

Step *1*

Step *2*

Step *3*

Chicken with Spicy Chick-Peas (Garbanzo Beans)

This delicious combination of spiced chick-peas and chicken uses canned chick-peas which speeds up the cooking time considerably.

SERVES 4

INGREDIENTS

3 tbsp ghee or vegetable oil
8 small chicken pieces
1 large onion, chopped
2 garlic cloves, crushed
1–2 fresh green chillies, seeded and chopped,
or use 1–2 tsp minced chilli (from a jar)
2 tsp ground cumin
2 tsp ground coriander
1 tsp garam masala
1 tsp ground turmeric
425 g/14 oz can chopped tomatoes
150 ml/¼ pint/⅔ cup water
1 tbsp chopped fresh mint
475 g/15 oz can chick-peas (garbazo beans), drained
salt
1 tbsp chopped fresh coriander (cilantro)
natural yogurt (optional), to serve

1 Heat the ghee or oil in a large saucepan and fry the chicken pieces all over until sealed and lightly golden.

2 Remove from the pan. Add the onion, garlic, chilli and spices and cook very gently for 2 minutes, stirring frequently.

3 Stir in the tomatoes, water, mint and chick-peas (garbanzo beans). Mix well, return the chicken portions to the pan, season with salt to taste, then cover and simmer gently for about 20 minutes or until the chicken is tender and cooked through.

4 Taste and adjust the seasoning if necessary, then sprinkle with the chopped coriander (cilantro) and serve hot, drizzled with yogurt, if using.

Step *1*

Step *2*

Step *3*

Chicken Tikka Masala

Serve this very rich dish with an array of accompaniments to provide a balance and to neutralize the fiery flavours.

SERVES 4

INGREDIENTS

½ onion, chopped coarsely
60 g/2 oz/3 tbsp tomato purée (paste)
1 tsp cumin seeds
2.5 cm/1 inch piece ginger root, chopped
3 tbsp lemon juice
2 garlic cloves, crushed
2 tsp chilli powder
750 g/1½ lb boneless chicken
salt and pepper
fresh mint sprigs, to garnish

MASALA SAUCE

2 tbsp ghee
1 onion, sliced
1 tbsp black onion seeds
3 garlic cloves, crushed
2 fresh green chillies, chopped
200 g/7 oz can tomatoes
120 ml/4 fl oz/½ cup natural yogurt
120 ml/4 fl oz/½ cup coconut milk
1 tbsp chopped fresh coriander (cilantro)
1 tbsp chopped fresh mint
2 tbsp lemon or lime juice
½ tsp garam masala

1 Purée the onion, tomato purée (paste), cumin, ginger, lemon juice, garlic, chilli powder and salt and pepper in a food processor or blender and then transfer to a bowl. Alternatively, grind the cumin in a pestle and mortar and transfer to a bowl. Finely chop the onion and ginger and stir into the bowl with the tomato purée (paste), lemon juice, salt and pepper, garlic and chilli powder.

2 Cut chicken into 4 cm/1¼ inch cubes. Stir into the bowl and leave to marinate for 2 hours.

3 Make the masala sauce. Heat the ghee in a large saucepan, add the onion and stir over a medium heat for 5 minutes. Add the onion seeds, garlic and chillies and cook until fragrant.

4 Add the tomatoes, yogurt and coconut milk, bring to the boil, then simmer for 20 minutes.

5 Meanwhile, divide the chicken evenly between 8 oiled skewers and cook under a preheated very hot grill (broiler) for 15 minutes, turning frequently. Remove the chicken from the skewers and add to the sauce. Stir in the fresh coriander (cilantro), mint, lemon or lime juice, and garam masala. Serve garnished with mint sprigs.

Step *1*

Step *2*

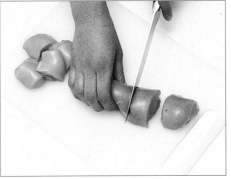

Step *3*

Shahi Murg

Shahi Murg is a traditional curry cooked in yogurt by a slow-cooking method that is used to make many of the sauces in India.

SERVES 4

INGREDIENTS

1 tsp cumin seeds
1 tsp coriander seeds
2 tbsp ghee
1 onion, sliced finely
8 chicken pieces
½ tsp salt
350 ml/12 fl oz/1½ cups natural yogurt
120 ml/4 fl oz/½ cup double (heavy) cream
1 tbsp ground almonds
½ tsp garam masala
3 cloves
seeds from 3 green cardamom pods
1 bay leaf
60 g/2 oz/⅓ cup sultanas (golden raisins)
fresh coriander (cilantro) sprigs, to garnish

1 Grind together the cumin and coriander seeds in a spice grinder or a pestle and mortar.

2 Heat half the ghee in a large saucepan and cook the onion over a medium heat for 15 minutes, stirring occasionally, until the onion is very soft and sweet.

3 Meanwhile, heat the remaining ghee in a large frying pan (skillet) and brown the chicken pieces well. Add to the onions.

4 Add the ground cumin and coriander, salt, yogurt, cream, almonds and garam masala.

5 Bring to a gentle simmer, and add the cloves, cardamom, bay leaf and sultanas (golden raisins).

6 Simmer for 40 minutes until the chicken juices run clear when the thickest part of each piece is pierced with a sharp knife, and the sauce has reduced and thickened.

7 Serve garnished with coriander (cilantro) sprigs.

Step *1*

Step *3*

Step *4*

Stir-Fry Chicken Curry

*A tasty mix of chicken, peppers and cashew nuts is stir-fried with
spices to give a delicious dish in minutes.*

SERVES 4

INGREDIENTS

4 boneless chicken breasts, skinned
6 tbsp strained thick yogurt
2 tbsp lime juice
2 garlic cloves, crushed
5 cm/2 inch piece ginger root, chopped
2 tbsp medium or hot curry paste, or to taste
1 tbsp paprika
5 tbsp ghee or vegetable oil
1 onion, quartered
and separated into layers
1 red (bell) pepper, seeded and cut into
1 cm/½ inch pieces
1 green (bell) pepper, seeded and
cut into 1 cm/½ inch pieces
60 g/2 oz/½ cup unsalted cashews
4 tbsp water
salt
snipped chives or spring onion
(scallion) tops, to garnish

1 Cut the chicken breasts into 1 cm/½ inch wide strips and place in a bowl. Add the yogurt, lime juice, garlic, ginger, curry paste and paprika. Season well and mix the ingredients together.

2 Heat the ghee or oil in a large frying pan, add the onion, red and green (bell) peppers and the cashews and stir-fry over a moderate heat for 2 minutes. Remove from the pan and reserve.

3 Stir the chicken mixture into the pan and stir-fry for 4–5 minutes until well sealed and cooked though.

4 Add the water and mix well, then return the vegetables to the pan, reduce the heat and cook gently for 2 minutes. Serve at once, sprinkled with chives or spring onion (scallion) tops.

Step *1*

Step *3*

Step *4*

Chicken & Vegetable Rice

Boneless chicken breasts may be used here instead of the drumsticks, if
preferred, in which case slash them diagonally through the flesh.

SERVES 4–6

INGREDIENTS

4 chicken drumsticks
3 tbsp mango chutney
1½ tbsp lemon juice
6 tbsp vegetable oil
1½–2 tbsp medium or hot curry paste
1½ tsp paprika
1 large onion, chopped
125 g/4 oz button mushrooms,
wiped and left whole
2 carrots, peeled and sliced thinly
2 celery sticks, trimmed and sliced thinly
½ aubergine (eggplant),
quartered and sliced
2 garlic cloves, crushed
½ tsp ground cinnamon
250 g/8 oz/1¼ cups long-grain rice
600 ml/1 pint/2½ cups chicken stock or water
60 g/2 oz frozen peas or sliced French (green) beans
60 g/2 oz/⅓ cup seedless raisins
salt and pepper

TO GARNISH

wedges of hard-boiled egg
lemon slices

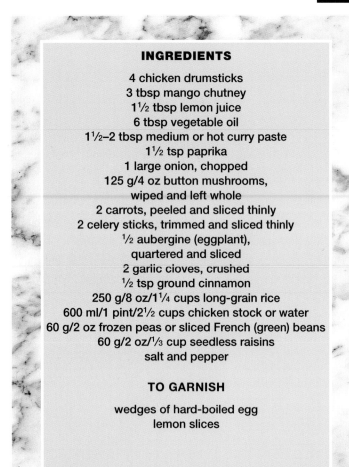

1 Slash the drumsticks twice on each side, cutting through the skin and deep into the flesh each time. Mix the chutney with the lemon juice, 1 tablespoon oil, curry paste and paprika. Brush over the drumsticks and reserve the remainder for later.

2 Heat 2 tablespoons of oil in the frying pan and fry the drumsticks over a moderate heat for about 5 minutes until sealed and golden brown all over.

3 Meanwhile, heat the remaining oil in a saucepan, add the onion, mushrooms, carrots, celery, aubergine (eggplant), garlic and cinnamon and fry lightly for 1 minute. Stir in the rice and cook gently for 1 minute, stirring until the rice is well coated with the oil. Add the stock or water and the remaining mango chutney mixture, peas or French (green) beans, raisins, and salt and pepper to taste. Bring to the boil.

4 Reduce the heat and add the drumsticks to the mixture, pushing them down into the liquid. Cover and cook gently for 25 minutes until the liquid has been absorbed and the drumsticks are tender.

5 Remove the drumsticks from the pan and keep warm. Fluff up the rice mixture and transfer to a warm serving plate. Arrange the rice into a nicely shaped mound and place the drumsticks around it. Garnish the dish with wedges of hard-boiled egg and lemon slices.

Step *1*

Step *3*

Step *4*

Balti Chicken Paneer

This recipe is based on one of the most popular Balti recipes, chicken in butter sauce. The poppy seeds in the sauce enhance the nutty taste of the almonds.

SERVES 4

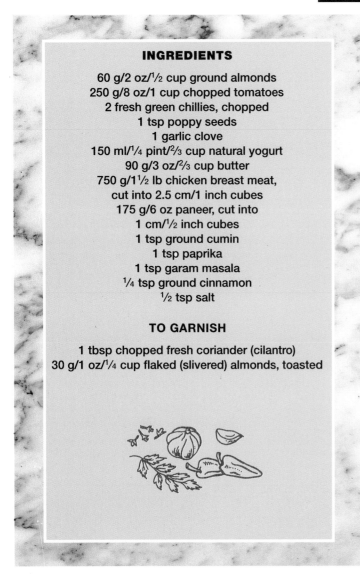

INGREDIENTS

60 g/2 oz/½ cup ground almonds
250 g/8 oz/1 cup chopped tomatoes
2 fresh green chillies, chopped
1 tsp poppy seeds
1 garlic clove
150 ml/¼ pint/⅔ cup natural yogurt
90 g/3 oz/⅔ cup butter
750 g/1½ lb chicken breast meat,
cut into 2.5 cm/1 inch cubes
175 g/6 oz paneer, cut into
1 cm/½ inch cubes
1 tsp ground cumin
1 tsp paprika
1 tsp garam masala
¼ tsp ground cinnamon
½ tsp salt

TO GARNISH

1 tbsp chopped fresh coriander (cilantro)
30 g/1 oz/¼ cup flaked (slivered) almonds, toasted

1 Put the ground almonds, tomatoes, chillies, poppy seeds and garlic in a food processor or blender and blend to a smooth paste. Alternatively, push the tomatoes through a sieve (strainer), finely chop the chillies and garlic, crush the poppy seeds, then mix together the tomatoes, chillies, garlic, poppy seeds and ground almonds. Stir the yogurt into the tomato mixture.

2 Heat the butter in a karahi or wok, add the chicken and stir-fry for 5 minutes.

3 Add the paneer, cumin, paprika, garam masala, cinnamon and salt and stir-fry for 1 minute.

4 Add the tomato and yogurt mixture slowly to prevent the yogurt curdling. Simmer for 10–15 minutes until the chicken juices run clear when the chicken is pierced with a sharp knife.

5 Serve garnished with the coriander (cilantro) and flaked (slivered) almonds.

Step *1*

Step *3*

Step *4*

Chicken in Spiced Coconut Cream

This delicious combination would make a perfect dinner or supper party main course – and what's more it is quick and simple to prepare.

SERVES 4

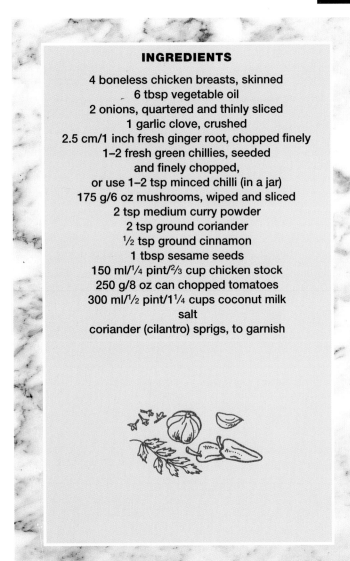

INGREDIENTS

4 boneless chicken breasts, skinned
6 tbsp vegetable oil
2 onions, quartered and thinly sliced
1 garlic clove, crushed
2.5 cm/1 inch fresh ginger root, chopped finely
1–2 fresh green chillies, seeded
and finely chopped,
or use 1–2 tsp minced chilli (in a jar)
175 g/6 oz mushrooms, wiped and sliced
2 tsp medium curry powder
2 tsp ground coriander
½ tsp ground cinnamon
1 tbsp sesame seeds
150 ml/¼ pint/⅔ cup chicken stock
250 g/8 oz can chopped tomatoes
300 ml/½ pint/1¼ cups coconut milk
salt
coriander (cilantro) sprigs, to garnish

1 Cut each chicken breast into 3 diagonal pieces. Heat 4 tablespoons of oil in a saucepan and fry the chicken pieces until lightly sealed all over. Remove from the pan and reserve.

2 Add the remaining oil to the pan and gently fry the onions, garlic, ginger, chillies, mushrooms, curry powder, spices and sesame seeds for 3 minutes, stirring frequently.

3 Stir in the chicken stock, tomatoes and coconut milk. Season with salt to taste and bring to the boil.

4 Reduce the heat, return the chicken pieces to the pan and simmer gently, uncovered, for about 12 minutes, or until the chicken is tender and cooked through and the sauce has thickened, stirring occasionally. Garnish with coriander (cilantro) sprigs.

Step *2*

Step *3*

Step *4*

Saffron Chicken

*This is a beautifully aromatic dish, the full fragrance of which brings to
mind the opulent days of the maharajahs.*

SERVES 4

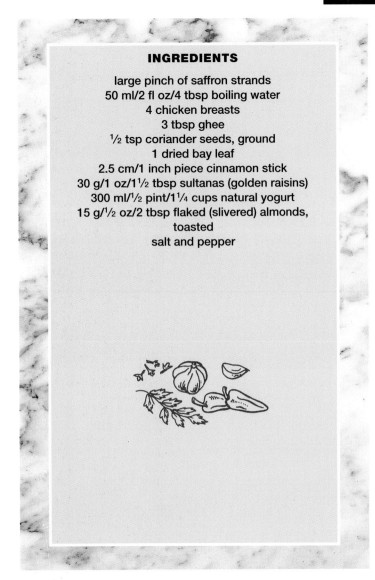

INGREDIENTS

large pinch of saffron strands
50 ml/2 fl oz/4 tbsp boiling water
4 chicken breasts
3 tbsp ghee
½ tsp coriander seeds, ground
1 dried bay leaf
2.5 cm/1 inch piece cinnamon stick
30 g/1 oz/1½ tbsp sultanas (golden raisins)
300 ml/½ pint/1¼ cups natural yogurt
15 g/½ oz/2 tbsp flaked (slivered) almonds,
toasted
salt and pepper

1 Combine the saffron with the boiling water, and leave to steep for 10 minutes.

2 Season the chicken pieces with salt and pepper.

3 Heat the ghee in a large frying pan (skillet), add the chicken pieces and brown on both sides. Cook in batches if necessary. Remove the chicken from the pan.

4 Reduce the heat to medium and add the coriander to the pan, stir once then add the bay leaf, cinnamon stick, sultanas (golden raisins) and the saffron with the soaking water, all at once.

5 Return the chicken to the pan. Cover and simmer gently for 40–50 minutes or until the chicken juices run clear when the thickest part of each piece is pierced with a sharp knife. Remove the pan from the heat and gently stir the yogurt into the sauce.

6 Discard the bay leaf and cinnamon stick. Scatter over the toasted almonds and serve.

Step *1*

Step *2*

Step *3*

Karahi Chicken

A karahi is an extremely versatile two-handled metal pan, similar to a wok. Food is always cooked over a high heat in a karahi.

SERVES 4–6

INGREDIENTS

2 tbsp ghee
3 garlic cloves, crushed
1 onion, chopped finely
2 tbsp garam masala
1 tsp coriander seeds, ground
½ tsp dried mint
1 bay leaf
750 g/1½ lb boneless chicken meat, diced
200 ml/7 fl oz/scant 1 cup chicken stock
1 tbsp chopped fresh coriander (cilantro)
salt
naan bread or chapatis, to serve

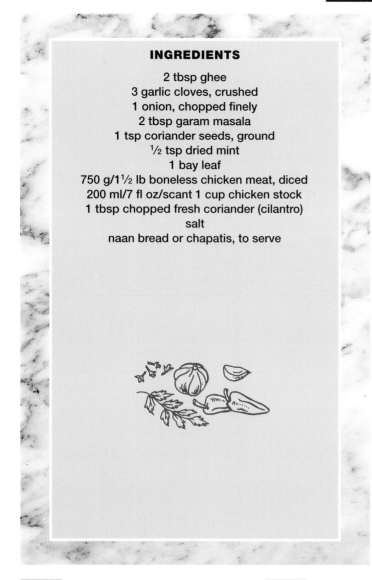

1 Heat the ghee in a karahi, wok, or a large, heavy frying pan (skillet) and add the garlic and onion. Stir for about 4 minutes until the onion is golden.

2 Stir in the garam masala, ground coriander, mint and bay leaf.

3 Add the chicken and cook over a high heat, stirring occasionally, for about 5 minutes.

4 Add the stock and simmer for 10 minutes, until the sauce has thickened and the chicken juices run clear when the meat is tested with a sharp knife.

5 Stir in the fresh coriander (cilantro), salt to taste and serve immediately with naan bread or chapatis.

Step *1*

Step *3*

Step *4*

Chicken & Aromatic Almonds

*Rich and delicious – enjoy the succulence of chicken cooked with yogurt,
cream and ground almonds flavoured with aromatic garam masala.*

SERVES 4

INGREDIENTS

150 ml/¼ pint/⅔ cup thick yogurt
½ tsp cornflour (cornstarch)
4 tbsp ghee or vegetable oil
4 boneless chicken breasts
2 onions, sliced
1 garlic clove, crushed
2.5 cm/1 inch piece fresh root ginger,
chopped finely
1½ tbsp garam masala
½ tsp chilli powder
2 tsp medium curry paste
300 ml/½ pint/1¼ cups chicken stock
150 ml/¼ pint/⅔ cup double (heavy) cream
60 g/2 oz/½ cup ground almonds
125 g/4 oz French (green) beans,
trimmed and halved
2 tbsp lemon juice
salt and pepper
flaked (slivered) almonds, toasted, to garnish
boiled rice, to serve

1 Smoothly blend the yogurt in a small bowl with the cornflour (cornstarch). Heat the ghee or oil in a large flameproof casserole. Add the chicken breasts and fry until golden all over. Remove the chicken from the casserole and reserve.

2 Add the onions, garlic and ginger to the casserole and fry gently for 3 minutes, then add the garam masala, chilli powder and curry paste and fry gently for 1 minute. Stir in the stock, yogurt, and salt and pepper to taste and bring to the boil, stirring all the time.

3 Return the chicken breasts to the casserole, then cover and simmer gently for 25 minutes. Remove the chicken to a dish and keep warm.

4 Blend the cream with the ground almonds and add to the sauce. Stir in the green beans and lemon juice and boil vigorously for 1 minute, stirring all the time.

5 Return the chicken to the casserole, cover and cook gently for a further 10 minutes. Garnish with toasted flaked (slivered) almonds and serve with rice.

Step *2*

Step *4*

Step *5*

MEAT DISHES

Curries are, of course, the most famous of Indian meat dishes, but they are by no means the only dishes the Indian culinary repertoire has to offer! Consider stir-fries with a blend of Indian spices, skewered kebabs of meat and vegetables, vegetables stuffed with savoury meat and rice or lentil mixtures, risotto-style combinations of meat with rice, or meat roasted tandoori-style.

Even then there are differences and variations which give a typical national dish a distinctive regional flavour all of its own. South India curries, for example, are fierce and fiery, while North Kashmiri and Punjab meat dishes are comparatively mild and flavoured with onion and garlic. Western or Goan dishes are slow-cooked, hot and thickened with coconut milk, whereas Eastern meat dishes rely upon spices such as mustard, cumin and anise for their distinctive flavour and originality.

Meat dishes often incorporate vegetables to make a complete meal in one pan. This type of dish is ideal when cooking a quick evening meal, as you only need to serve naan bread or chapatis as an accompaniment: it also saves on the washing up.

Masala Lamb & Lentils

This recipe makes a good warming winter curry.
Gram lentils have been used here but you could use split yellow peas.

SERVES 4

INGREDIENTS

2 tbsp oil
1 tsp cumin seeds
2 bay leaves
2.5 cm/1 inch piece cinnamon stick
1 onion, chopped
750 g/1½ lb lean, boneless lamb,
cut into 2.5 cm/1 inch cubes
125 g/4 oz/½ cup split gram lentils,
soaked for 6 hours and drained
1 tsp salt
1 fresh green chilli, sliced
1.25 litres/2¼ pints/5 cups water
1 garlic clove, crushed
¼ tsp ground turmeric
1 tsp chilli powder
½ tsp garam masala
1 tbsp chopped fresh coriander (cilantro)

1 Heat the oil in a karahi or wok and add the cumin seeds, bay leaves and cinnamon and fry until the seeds start popping.

2 Add the onion to the pan and stir-fry until golden brown.

3 Stir the lamb into the onion and stir-fry until browned.

4 Add the lentils, salt, chilli, water, garlic, turmeric and chilli powder. Bring to the boil, then simmer for 1 hour until the meat and lentils are tender.

5 Taste and stir the garam masala into the pan, and cook for a further 5 minutes. Stir in the coriander (cilantro), and serve.

Step *1*

Step *3*

Step *4*

Lamb Tikka Masala

This is a very rich dish, and is best enjoyed with simple accompaniments, such as dal, naan bread, a salad and some plain basmati rice.

SERVES 6

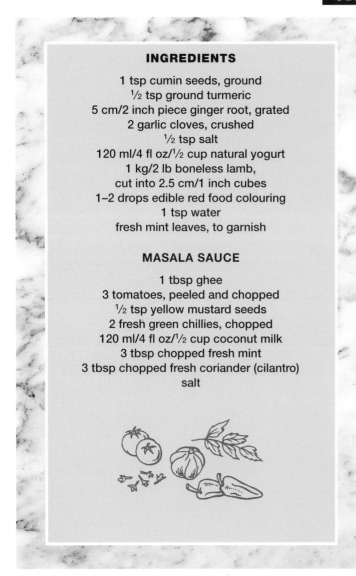

INGREDIENTS

1 tsp cumin seeds, ground
½ tsp ground turmeric
5 cm/2 inch piece ginger root, grated
2 garlic cloves, crushed
½ tsp salt
120 ml/4 fl oz/½ cup natural yogurt
1 kg/2 lb boneless lamb,
cut into 2.5 cm/1 inch cubes
1–2 drops edible red food colouring
1 tsp water
fresh mint leaves, to garnish

MASALA SAUCE

1 tbsp ghee
3 tomatoes, peeled and chopped
½ tsp yellow mustard seeds
2 fresh green chillies, chopped
120 ml/4 fl oz/½ cup coconut milk
3 tbsp chopped fresh mint
3 tbsp chopped fresh coriander (cilantro)
salt

1 Combine the cumin, turmeric, ginger, garlic, salt and yogurt in a bowl. Stir in the lamb until evenly coated with the sauce. Dilute the food colouring with the water, and add to the bowl, stirring well. Marinate in the refrigerator for 2 hours. Soak 6 wooden skewers in warm water for 15 minutes.

2 Make the masala sauce. Heat the ghee in a large saucepan and add the tomatoes, mustard seeds, green chillies and coconut milk. Bring to the boil, then simmer for 20 minutes until the tomatoes have broken down. Stir occasionally.

3 Thread the pieces of lamb on to 6 oiled skewers. Set on a grill (broiler) pan and cook under a preheated very hot grill for 15–20 minutes, turning occasionally.

4 Stir the mint and fresh coriander (cilantro) into the sauce, and season with salt.

5 Carefully remove the lamb from the skewers. Stir the lamb into the sauce and serve garnished with mint leaves.

Step *1*

Step *3*

Step *5*

Lamb Pasanda

This dish is as close as one gets to the classic curry that springs to mind
when Indian cooking is mentioned.

SERVES 4

INGREDIENTS

500 g/1 lb boneless lamb
150 ml/¼ pint/⅔ cup red wine
75 ml/3 fl oz/⅛ cup oil
3 garlic cloves, crushed
5 cm/2 inch piece ginger root, grated
1 tsp coriander seeds, ground
1 tsp cumin seeds, ground
2 tbsp ghee
1 large onion, chopped
1 tsp garam masala
2 fresh green chillies, halved
300 ml/½ pint/1¼ cups natural yogurt
2 tbsp ground almonds
20 whole blanched almonds
salt

1 Cut the lamb into strips 2.5 cm/1 inch across and 10 cm/4 inches long. Set aside.

2 Combine the red wine, oil, garlic, ginger, ground coriander and cumin seeds in a large non-metallic bowl. Stir in the lamb and leave to marinate for 1 hour.

3 Heat the ghee in a frying pan (skillet) and fry the onion until brown.

4 Drain the lamb, reserving the contents of the bowl. Pat the lamb dry with paper towels. Add the lamb to the frying pan (skillet) and stir over a high heat until it is evenly sealed and browned.

5 Add the contents of the bowl to the pan, and bring to a gentle boil. Add the garam masala, chillies, yogurt, ground almonds, whole almonds, and salt to taste. Cover and simmer for 12–15 minutes until the lamb is tender.

Step *3*

Step *4*

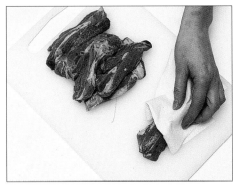

Step *5*

Lamb & Potato Masala

It's so easy to create delicious Indian dishes at home – simply open a can
of curry sauce and add a few interesting ingredients.

SERVES 4

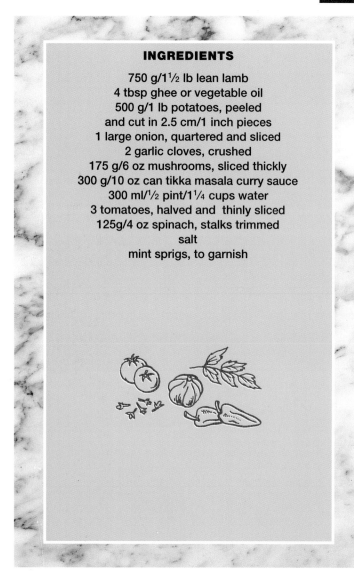

INGREDIENTS

750 g/1½ lb lean lamb
4 tbsp ghee or vegetable oil
500 g/1 lb potatoes, peeled
and cut in 2.5 cm/1 inch pieces
1 large onion, quartered and sliced
2 garlic cloves, crushed
175 g/6 oz mushrooms, sliced thickly
300 g/10 oz can tikka masala curry sauce
300 ml/½ pint/1¼ cups water
3 tomatoes, halved and thinly sliced
125g/4 oz spinach, stalks trimmed
salt
mint sprigs, to garnish

1 Cut the lamb into 2.5 cm/1 inch cubes. Heat the ghee or oil in a large pan, add the lamb and fry over moderate heat for 3 minutes or until sealed all over. Remove from the pan.

2 Add the potatoes, onion, garlic and mushrooms and fry for 3–4 minutes, stirring frequently. Stir the curry sauce and water into the pan, add the lamb, mix well and season with salt to taste. Cover and cook very gently for 1 hour or until the lamb is tender and cooked through, stirring occasionally.

3 Add the tomatoes and spinach to the pan, pushing the leaves well down into the mixture. Cover and cook for a further 10 minutes until the spinach is tender. Garnish with mint sprigs and serve hot.

Step *1*

Step *2*

Step *2*

Lamb Do Pyaza

*Do Pyaza usually indicates a dish of meat cooked with plenty of onions,
and in this recipe the onions are cooked in two different ways.*

SERVES 4

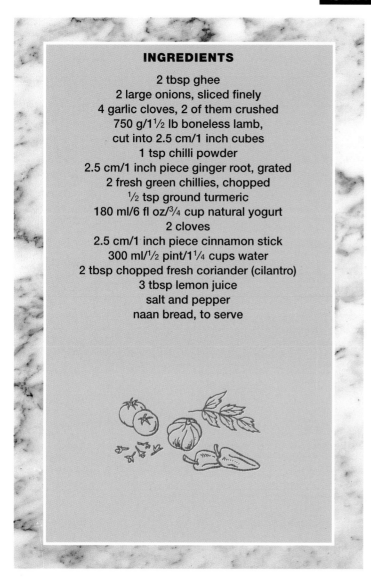

INGREDIENTS

2 tbsp ghee
2 large onions, sliced finely
4 garlic cloves, 2 of them crushed
750 g/1½ lb boneless lamb,
cut into 2.5 cm/1 inch cubes
1 tsp chilli powder
2.5 cm/1 inch piece ginger root, grated
2 fresh green chillies, chopped
½ tsp ground turmeric
180 ml/6 fl oz/¾ cup natural yogurt
2 cloves
2.5 cm/1 inch piece cinnamon stick
300 ml/½ pint/1¼ cups water
2 tbsp chopped fresh coriander (cilantro)
3 tbsp lemon juice
salt and pepper
naan bread, to serve

1 Heat the ghee in a large saucepan and add 1 of the onions and all the garlic. Cook for 2–3 minutes, stirring constantly.

2 Add the lamb and brown all over. Remove and set aside.

3 Add the chilli powder, ginger, chillies and turmeric and stir for a further 30 seconds.

4 Add plenty of salt and pepper, the yogurt, cloves, cinnamon and water. Return the lamb to the pan. Bring to the boil then simmer for 10 minutes.

5 Transfer to an ovenproof dish and cook uncovered in a preheated oven, 180°C/350°F/Gas Mark 4, for 40 minutes. Check the seasoning.

6 Stir in the remaining onion and cook uncovered for a further 40 minutes.

7 Add the fresh coriander (cilantro) and lemon juice. Serve with naan bread.

Step *1*

Step *3*

Step *6*

Rogan Josh

Rogan Josh is one of the best-known curries and is a great favourite in restaurants. The title means 'red curry', the red being provided by the chillies.

SERVES 6

INGREDIENTS

2 tbsp ghee
1 kg/2 lb braising steak,
cut into 2.5 cm/1 inch cubes
1 onion, chopped finely
3 garlic cloves
2.5 cm/1 inch piece ginger root, grated
4 fresh red chillies, chopped
4 green cardamom pods
4 cloves
2 tsp coriander seeds
2 tsp cumin seeds
1 tsp paprika
1 tsp salt
1 bay leaf
120 ml /4 fl oz/¼ cup natural yogurt
2.5 cm/1 inch piece cinnamon stick
150 ml/¼ pint/⅔ cups hot water
¼ tsp garam masala
pepper

1 Heat the ghee in a large flameproof casserole and brown the meat in batches. Set aside in a bowl.

2 Add the onion to the ghee and stir over a high heat for 3–4 minutes.

3 Grind together the garlic, ginger, chillies, cardamom, cloves, coriander, cumin, paprika and salt.

4 Add the spice paste and bay leaf to the casserole and stir until fragrant.

5 Return the meat and any juices in the bowl to the casserole and simmer for 2–3 minutes.

6 Gradually stir the yogurt into the casserole keeping the sauce simmering.

7 Stir in the cinnamon and hot water, and pepper to taste.

8 Cover the casserole and cook in a preheated oven, 180°C/350°F/Gas Mark 4, for 1¼ hours, stirring frequently, until the meat is very tender and the sauce is slightly reduced.

9 Discard the cinnamon stick and stir in the garam masala. Remove surplus oil from the surface of the casserole before serving.

Step *2*

Step *4*

Step *7*

Lamb Phall

*Do try to use freshly ground whole spices for this delicious hot curry, as
they will make the overall taste more complex and enjoyable.*

SERVES 4–6

INGREDIENTS

8 fresh or dried red chillies, or to taste
4 tbsp ghee
1 onion, chopped finely
6 garlic cloves, chopped finely
5 cm/2 inch piece ginger root, chopped finely
1 tsp cumin seeds, ground
1 tsp coriander seeds, ground
1 tsp fenugreek seeds, ground
1 tsp garam masala
425 g/14 oz can tomatoes
1 tbsp tomato ketchup
1 tbsp tomato purée (paste)
750 g/1½ lb boneless lamb
cut into 5 cm/2 inch cubes

TO SERVE

Cucumber Raita (page 234)
pickles

1 Chop 4 of the chillies and leave the other 4 whole.

2 Heat half of the ghee in a saucepan and add the onion, garlic and ginger. Stir over a medium heat until golden.

3 Stir the cumin, coriander, fenugreek and garam masala into the onion mixture. Cook over a medium heat for 10 minutes.

4 Stir the canned tomatoes, tomato ketchup, tomato purée (paste) and the whole and chopped chillies into the pan, and bring to a gentle boil. Cook over a low heat for 10 minutes.

5 Meanwhile, heat the remaining ghee in a flameproof casserole and cook the meat until evenly sealed. Cook in batches if necessary.

6 Transfer the sauce to the casserole with the meat, cover and cook in a preheated oven, 180°C/350°F/Gas Mark 4, for 1½ hours until the meat is tender.

7 Serve with cucumber raita and pickles.

Step 2

Step 3

Step 4

Lamb Bhuna

The pungent flavours of the chillies in this curry should not hide the flavours of the other spices.

SERVES 4–6

INGREDIENTS

1 onion, chopped
2 garlic cloves
3 tomatoes, peeled and chopped
1 tsp malt vinegar
1 tbsp oil
750 g/1½ lb lean boneless lamb, cut into
4 cm/1½ inch cubes
2 tsp coriander seeds, ground
1 tsp cumin seeds, ground
2 dried red chillies, chopped
3 fresh green chillies, chopped
½ tsp ground turmeric
30 g/1 oz/2 tbsp creamed coconut
50 ml/2 fl oz/4 tbsp water
1 tsp garam masala
salt and pepper
fresh coriander (cilantro) leaves, to garnish

1 Purée the onion, garlic, tomatoes and vinegar in a food processor or blender. Alternatively, chop the vegetables finely by hand, then mix with the vinegar. Set aside.

2 Heat the oil in a large frying pan (skillet) and brown the meat for 5–10 minutes. Remove and set aside.

3 Reduce the heat and add the ground coriander seeds, cumin, chillies and turmeric to the pan. Stir continuously until the spices are fragrant.

4 Increase the heat again and add the onion mixture. Stir-fry for 5 minutes until nearly dry.

5 Return the meat to the pan. Combine the coconut and water and add to the pan. Simmer for 45–60 minutes until the meat is tender. Stir in the garam masala and season to taste.

6 Serve garnished with fresh coriander (cilantro) leaves.

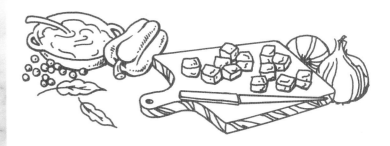

Step *1*

Step *3*

Step *5*

Spicy Beef & Yogurt

Deliciously quick and easy – stir-fried steak is served with a tangy aubergine (eggplant) yogurt dressing. Use mild, medium or hot curry paste according to taste.

SERVES 4

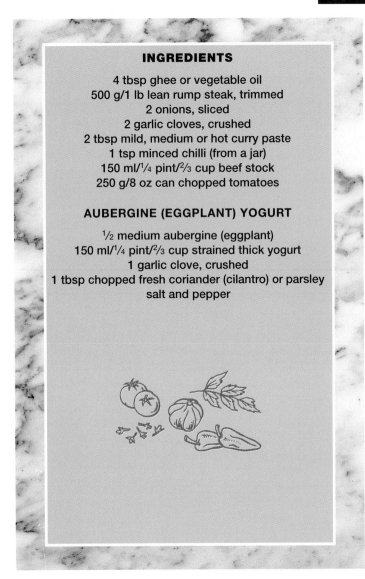

INGREDIENTS

4 tbsp ghee or vegetable oil
500 g/1 lb lean rump steak, trimmed
2 onions, sliced
2 garlic cloves, crushed
2 tbsp mild, medium or hot curry paste
1 tsp minced chilli (from a jar)
150 ml/¼ pint/⅔ cup beef stock
250 g/8 oz can chopped tomatoes

AUBERGINE (EGGPLANT) YOGURT

½ medium aubergine (eggplant)
150 ml/¼ pint/⅔ cup strained thick yogurt
1 garlic clove, crushed
1 tbsp chopped fresh coriander (cilantro) or parsley
salt and pepper

1 First make the aubergine (eggplant) yogurt. Peel the aubergine (eggplant) and cut into 2.5 cm/1 inch pieces. Place in the top half of a steamer and steam over boiling water for 10 minutes.

2 Meanwhile, whisk the yogurt with the garlic, coriander (cilantro), and salt and pepper to taste. Allow the cooked aubergine (eggplant) to cool slightly, then mash with a fork. Stir the aubergine (eggplant) into the yogurt.

3 Heat the ghee or oil in a large frying pan, add the beef and onions and stir-fry for 5 minutes until the beef is sealed all over.

4 Stir in the garlic, curry paste, chilli, stock and tomatoes and bring to the boil. Cover, reduce the heat and simmer gently for 5 minutes, stirring occasionally. Serve hot with the aubergine (eggplant) yogurt.

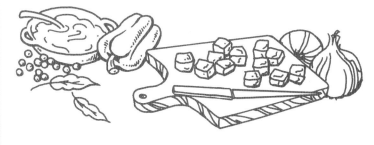

Step *1*

Step *3*

Step *4*

Beef & Mushroom Curry

Vary the meat here according to personal taste, using lean lamb or pork (leg or shoulder cuts are ideal) instead of beef. Omit the finishing touches (see step 4) if wished.

SERVES 4

INGREDIENTS

750 g/1½ lb lean braising beef, trimmed
3 tbsp vegetable oil
2 onions, sliced
2 garlic cloves, crushed
2.5 cm/1 inch piece ginger root,
chopped finely
2 fresh green chillies, seeded and chopped,
or use 1–2 tsp minced chilli (from a jar)
1½ tbsp medium curry paste
1 tsp ground coriander
175–250 g/6–8 oz mushrooms, sliced thickly
900 ml/1½ pints/3½ cups stock
3 tomatoes, chopped
½–1 tsp salt
60 g/2 oz creamed coconut, chopped
2 tbsp ground almonds

TO FINISH

2 tbsp vegetable oil
1 green or red (bell) pepper,
seeded and cut into thin strips
6 spring onions (scallions), trimmed and sliced
1 tsp cumin seeds

1 Cut the beef into small bite-sized cubes. Heat the oil in a saucepan, add the beef and fry until sealed, stirring frequently. Remove from the pan.

2 Add the onions, garlic, ginger, chillies, curry paste and coriander to the pan and cook gently for 2 minutes. Stir in the mushrooms, stock and tomatoes, and season with salt to taste. Return the beef to the pan, then cover and simmer very gently for 1¼ -1½ hours or until the beef is tender.

3 Stir the chopped creamed coconut and ground almonds into the curry, then cover the pan and cook gently for 3 minutes.

4 Meanwhile, heat the remaining oil in a frying pan, add the (bell) pepper strips and spring onion (scallion) slices and fry gently until glistening and tender-crisp. Stir in the cumin seeds and fry gently for 30 seconds, then spoon the mixture over the curry and serve at once.

Step *2*

Step *3*

Step *4*

Vindaloo Curry

*Vindaloo is the classic fiery curry that originates in Goa. The 'vin' in the
title refers to the vinegar that is added to tenderize the meat.*

SERVES 4–6

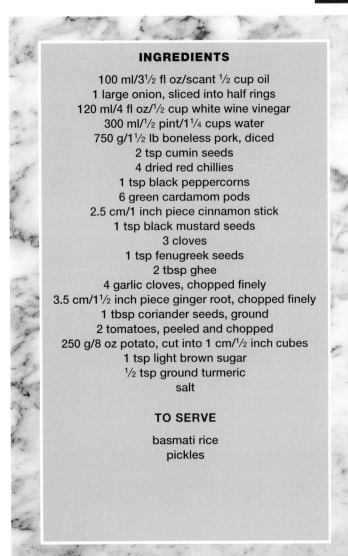

INGREDIENTS

100 ml/3½ fl oz/scant ½ cup oil
1 large onion, sliced into half rings
120 ml/4 fl oz/½ cup white wine vinegar
300 ml/½ pint/1¼ cups water
750 g/1½ lb boneless pork, diced
2 tsp cumin seeds
4 dried red chillies
1 tsp black peppercorns
6 green cardamom pods
2.5 cm/1 inch piece cinnamon stick
1 tsp black mustard seeds
3 cloves
1 tsp fenugreek seeds
2 tbsp ghee
4 garlic cloves, chopped finely
3.5 cm/1½ inch piece ginger root, chopped finely
1 tbsp coriander seeds, ground
2 tomatoes, peeled and chopped
250 g/8 oz potato, cut into 1 cm/½ inch cubes
1 tsp light brown sugar
½ tsp ground turmeric
salt

TO SERVE

basmati rice
pickles

1 Heat the oil in a large saucepan and fry the onion until golden brown. Set aside.

2 Combine 2 tablespoons of the vinegar with 1 tablespoon of the water in a large bowl. Add the pork and stir together well. Set aside.

3 In a food processor or blender mix the onions, cumin, chillies, peppercorns, cardamom, cinnamon, mustard seeds, cloves and fenugreek to a paste. Alternatively, grind the ingredients together in a pestle and mortar. Transfer to a bowl and add the remaining vinegar.

4 Heat the ghee in a frying pan (skillet) or casserole and cook the pork until it is browned on all sides.

5 Add the garlic, ginger and ground coriander and stir until fragrant, then add the tomatoes, potato, brown sugar, turmeric and remaining water. Add salt to taste and bring to the boil. Stir in the spice paste, cover and reduce the heat, and simmer for 1 hour until the pork is tender.

6 Serve with basmati rice and pickles.

Step *2*

Step *3*

Step *5*

Pork Chops & Spicy Red Beans

A tasty and substantial dish that is packed full of goodness. The spicy bean mixture,
served on its own, also makes a good accompaniment to meat or chicken dishes.

SERVES 4

INGREDIENTS

3 tbsp ghee or vegetable oil
4 pork chops, rind removed
2 onions, thinly sliced
2 garlic cloves, crushed
2 fresh green chillies, seeded and
chopped, or use 1–2 tsp minced chilli (from a jar)
2.5 cm/1 inch piece ginger root, chopped finely
1½ tsp cumin seeds
1½ tsp ground coriander
600 ml/1 pint/2½ cups stock
2 tbsp tomato purée (paste)
½ aubergine (eggplant), trimmed and
cut into 1 cm/½ inch dice
425 g/14 oz can red kidney beans, drained
4 tbsp double (heavy) cream
salt
coriander (cilantro) sprigs, to garnish

1 Heat the ghee or oil in a large frying pan, add the pork chops and fry until sealed and browned on both sides. Remove from the pan and reserve.

2 Add the sliced onions, garlic, chillies, ginger and spices and fry gently for 2 minutes. Stir in the stock, tomato purée (paste), aubergine (eggplant) and salt to taste.

3 Bring the mixture to the boil, place the chops on top, then cover and simmer gently over medium heat for 30 minutes, or until the chops are tender and cooked through.

4 Remove the chops for a moment and stir the red kidney beans and cream into the mixture. Return the chops to the pan, cover and heat through gently for 5 minutes. Taste and adjust the seasoning, if necessary. Serve hot, garnished with coriander (cilantro) sprigs.

Step *1*

Step *3*

Step *4*

VEGETABLE DISHES

*By applying myriad methods born of a centuries-old
tradition of vegetarianism, Indian cooks turn the
simplest vegetables into the most extraordinary feasts.
Many of these cooking methods are completely alien to
us, but they result in dishes which are both a joy to eat
and nourishing to the mind and body.*

*Indian vegetarianism is due mainly to the
predominant Hindu religion, with its reverence for
animals – especially cows – and its ideal of harmonizing
the diet with the need of the soul. A vegetarian diet is
followed also because vegetable growing is a more
efficient use of land than keeping animals for food.
Although we may be used to eating vegetables with
Indian meals in restaurants, restaurant cuisine
differs markedly from native cuisine. In India,
vegetables are relied on to play a leading role in a meal
– in a bhaji (a dry curry) for example,
or puréed in a bhartha.*

*Vegetable curries are flavoured simply, and the spices
and sauces can be easily transferred between
vegetables. For example, the sauce Palak Paneer
(page 160) can be used with other leafy vegetables, and
your own spice mixes experimented with when you have
some vegetables to cook.*

Vegetable Curry

*This colourful and interesting mixture of vegetables, cooked in a spicy
sauce, is excellent served with pilau rice and naan bread.*

SERVES 4

INGREDIENTS

250 g/8 oz turnips or swede, peeled
1 aubergine (eggplant), leaf end trimmed
350 g/12 oz new potatoes, scrubbed
250 g/8 oz cauliflower
250 g/8 oz button mushrooms, wiped
1 large onion
250 g/8 oz carrots, peeled
6 tbsp vegetable ghee or oil
2 garlic cloves, crushed
5 cm/2 inch ginger root, chopped finely
1–2 fresh green chillies, seeded and chopped
1 tbsp paprika
2 tsp ground coriander
1 tbsp mild or medium curry powder or paste
450 ml/³⁄₄ pint/1³⁄₄ cups vegetable stock
425 g/14 oz can chopped tomatoes
1 green (bell) pepper, seeded and sliced
15 ml/1 tbsp cornflour (cornstarch)
150 ml/¹⁄₄ pint/²⁄₃ cup coconut milk
2–3 tbsp ground almonds
salt
coriander (cilantro) sprigs, to garnish

1 Cut the turnips or swede, aubergine (eggplant) and potatoes into 1 cm (½ inch) cubes. Divide the cauliflower into small florets. Leave the mushrooms whole, or slice thickly, if preferred. Slice the onion and carrots.

2 Heat the ghee or oil in a large saucepan, add the onion, turnip, potato and cauliflower and cook gently for 3 minutes, stirring frequently. Add the garlic, ginger, chilli and spices and cook for 1 minute, stirring.

3 Add the stock, tomatoes, aubergine (eggplant) and mushrooms and season with salt. Cover and simmer gently for about 30 minutes or until tender, stirring occasionally. Add the green (bell) pepper, cover and continue cooking for a further 5 minutes.

4 Smoothly blend the cornflour (cornstarch) with the coconut milk and stir into the mixture. Add the ground almonds and simmer for 2 minutes, stirring all the time. Taste and adjust the seasoning, if necessary. Serve hot, garnished with coriander (cilantro) sprigs.

Step *1*

Step *2*

Step *3*

Mixed Vegetable Bhaji

In this delicious dish, the vegetables are first par-boiled and then lightly braised with onions, tomatoes and spices.

SERVES 4–6

INGREDIENTS

1 small cauliflower
125 g/4 oz French (green) beans
2 potatoes
4 tbsp ghee or vegetable oil
1 onion, chopped
2 garlic cloves, crushed
5 cm/2 inch ginger root, sliced thinly
1 tsp cumin seeds
2 tbsp medium curry paste
425 g/14 oz can chopped tomatoes
150 ml/¼ pint/⅔ cup water
4 tbsp strained thick yogurt
chopped fresh coriander (cilantro), to garnish

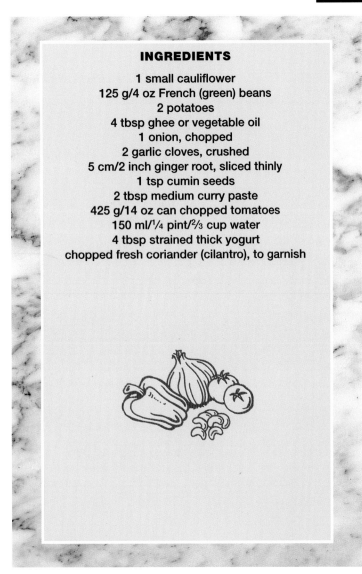

1 Break the cauliflower into neat florets. Top, tail and halve the beans. Peel and quarter the potatoes lengthways, then cut each quarter into 3 pieces. Cook all the prepared vegetables in a pan of boiling, salted water for 5 minutes. Drain the vegetables well, return to the pan and shake dry over a low heat for a few moments.

2 Heat the ghee or oil in a large frying pan, add the onion, garlic, ginger and cumin seeds and stir-fry gently for 3 minutes. Stir in the curry paste, tomatoes and water and bring to the boil. Reduce the heat and simmer the spicy mixture for 2 minutes.

3 Stir in the par-cooked vegetables and mix lightly. Cover and cook gently for 5–8 minutes until just tender and cooked through. Whisk the yogurt to soften and drizzle the vegetable mixture with the yogurt. Sprinkle with the chopped coriander (cilantro). Serve hot.

Step *1*

Step *2*

Step *3*

Brindil Bhaji

This is one of the most delicious of the bhaji dishes, and has a wonderful sweet spicy flavour.

SERVES 4

INGREDIENTS

500 g/1 lb aubergines (eggplant),
cut into 1 cm/½ inch slices
2 tbsp ghee
1 onion, sliced thinly
2 garlic cloves, sliced thinly
2.5 cm/1 inch piece ginger root, grated
½ tsp ground turmeric
1 dried red chilli
½ tsp salt
425 g/14 oz can tomatoes
1 tsp garam masala
fresh coriander (cilantro) sprigs, to garnish

1 Cut the aubergine (eggplant) slices into finger-width strips using a sharp knife.

2 Heat the ghee in a saucepan and cook the onion over a medium heat for 7–8 minutes, stirring constantly, until very soft.

3 Add the garlic and aubergine (eggplant), increase the heat and cook for 2 minutes.

4 Stir in the ginger, turmeric, chilli, salt and the tomatoes. Use the back of a wooden spoon to break up the tomatoes. Simmer uncovered for 15–20 minutes until the aubergine (eggplant) is very soft.

5 Stir in the garam masala. Simmer for a further 4–5 minutes.

6 Serve garnished with fresh coriander (cilantro) sprigs.

Step *1*

Step *2*

Step *4*

Roasted Aubergine (Eggplant) Curry

This is a rich vegetable dish, ideal served with a tandoori chicken and naan bread. Also delicious as a vegetarian dish with rice.

SERVES 6

INGREDIENTS

2 aubergines (eggplants)
250 ml/8 fl oz/1 cup natural yogurt
2 cardamom pods
½ tsp ground turmeric
1 dried red chilli
½ tsp coriander seeds
½ tsp pepper
1 tsp garam masala
1 clove
2 tbsp sunflower oil
1 onion, sliced lengthways
2 garlic cloves, crushed
1 tbsp grated ginger root
6 ripe tomatoes, peeled,
seeded and quartered
fresh coriander (cilantro), to garnish

1 Roast the aubergines (eggplants) in a very hot oven for 15 minutes, turning once, or over a naked flame, turning frequently, until charred and black all over. This should take about 5 minutes. Peel under running cold water. Cut off the stem end and discard.

2 Put the peeled aubergines (eggplants) into a large bowl and mash lightly with a fork. Stir in the yogurt. Set aside.

3 Grind together the cardamom pods, turmeric, red chilli, coriander seeds, pepper, garam masala and clove in a large pestle and mortar or spice grinder.

4 Heat the oil in a wok or heavy frying pan (skillet) over a moderate heat and cook the onion, garlic and ginger root until soft. Add the tomatoes and ground spices, and stir well.

5 Add the aubergine (eggplant) mixture to the pan and stir well. Cook for 5 minutes over a gentle heat, stirring constantly, until all the flavours are combined, and some of the liquid has evaporated. Serve immediately, garnished with coriander (cilantro).

Step *2*

Step *3*

Step *4*

Aubergine (Eggplant) in Saffron Sauce

*Here is a quick and simple, delicately spiced and delicious way
to cook aubergines (eggplant).*

SERVES 4

INGREDIENTS

a good pinch of saffron strands, crushed
1 tbsp boiling water
1 large aubergine (eggplant)
3 tbsp vegetable oil
1 large onion, coarsely chopped
2 garlic cloves, crushed
2.5 cm/1 inch ginger root, chopped
1½ tbsp mild or medium curry paste
1 tsp cumin seeds
150 ml/¼ pint/⅔ cup double (heavy) cream
150 ml/¼ pint/⅔ cup strained thick yogurt
2 tbsp mango chutney, chopped if necessary
salt and pepper

1 Place the saffron in a small bowl, add the boiling water and leave to infuse for 5 minutes.

2 Trim the leaf end off the aubergine (eggplant), cut lengthways into quarters, then into 1 cm/½ inch thick slices.

3 Heat the oil in a large frying pan, add the onion and cook gently for 3 minutes. Stir in the aubergine (eggplant), garlic, ginger, curry paste and cumin, and cook gently for 3 minutes.

4 Stir in the saffron solution, cream, yogurt and chutney, and cook gently for 8–10 minutes, stirring frequently, until the aubergine (eggplant) is cooked through and tender. Season with salt and pepper to taste and serve hot.

Step *2*

Step *3*

Step *4*

Aubergine (Eggplant) Bhaji

To make the panch poran spice mix, combine 2 tsp cumin seeds, 2 tsp mustard seeds, 2 tsp fennel seeds, ³/₄ tsp fenugreek and 1 tsp onion seeds.

SERVES 4

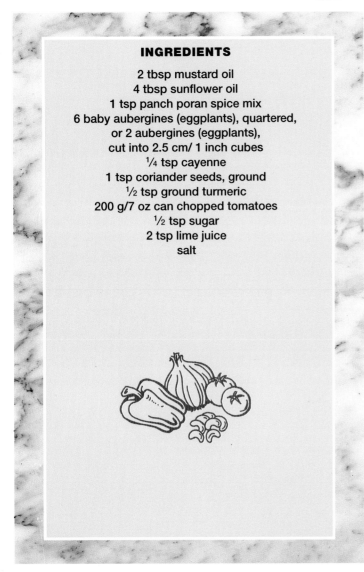

INGREDIENTS

2 tbsp mustard oil
4 tbsp sunflower oil
1 tsp panch poran spice mix
6 baby aubergines (eggplants), quartered,
or 2 aubergines (eggplants),
cut into 2.5 cm/ 1 inch cubes
¹/₄ tsp cayenne
1 tsp coriander seeds, ground
¹/₂ tsp ground turmeric
200 g/7 oz can chopped tomatoes
¹/₂ tsp sugar
2 tsp lime juice
salt

1 Heat the mustard oil in a wok or large frying pan (skillet) until it just starts to smoke. Reduce the heat and add the sunflower oil. Add the panch poran mix, stir once and add the aubergine (eggplant).

2 Add the cayenne, coriander and turmeric, and stir over a high heat for 2–3 minutes until the aubergine (eggplant) is sealed on all sides.

3 Add the chopped tomatoes and their juice to the pan and bring to the boil.

4 Simmer for 15 minutes or until the bhaji is nearly dry. Stir once or twice. Remove from the heat and stir in the sugar, the lime juice and a pinch of salt.

5 Transfer to a warmed serving dish, and serve immediately.

Step *1*

Step *3*

Step *4*

Long Beans with Tomatoes

Many Indian meals need some green vegetables to complement the spicy dishes and to set off the rich sauces.

SERVES 4–6

INGREDIENTS

500 g/1 lb green beans, cut into 5 cm/
2 inch lengths
2 tbsp ghee
2.5 cm/1 inch piece ginger root, grated
1 garlic clove, crushed
1 tsp ground turmeric
½ tsp cayenne
1 tsp ground coriander
4 tomatoes, peeled, seeded and diced
150 ml/¼ pint/⅔ cup vegetable stock

1 Blanch the beans quickly in boiling water, drain and refresh under cold running water.

2 Melt the ghee in a large saucepan. Add the grated ginger root and crushed garlic, stir and add the turmeric, cayenne and coriander. Stir until fragrant, about 1 minute.

3 Add the tomatoes, tossing them until they are thoroughly coated in the spice mix.

4 Add the vegetable stock to the pan, bring to the boil and cook over a medium-high heat for 10 minutes, until the sauce has thickened, stirring occasionally.

5 Add the beans, reduce the heat to moderate and heat through for 5 minutes, stirring.

6 Transfer to a serving dish and serve immediately.

Step *1*

Step *3*

Step *4*

Okra Bhaji

*This is a very mild-tasting, rich curry, which would be an ideal
accompaniment to a tomato-based main-course curry.*

SERVES 4

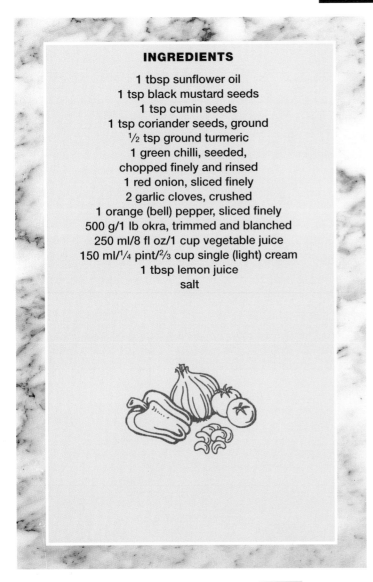

INGREDIENTS

1 tbsp sunflower oil
1 tsp black mustard seeds
1 tsp cumin seeds
1 tsp coriander seeds, ground
½ tsp ground turmeric
1 green chilli, seeded,
chopped finely and rinsed
1 red onion, sliced finely
2 garlic cloves, crushed
1 orange (bell) pepper, sliced finely
500 g/1 lb okra, trimmed and blanched
250 ml/8 fl oz/1 cup vegetable juice
150 ml/¼ pint/⅔ cup single (light) cream
1 tbsp lemon juice
salt

1 Heat the oil in a wok or large frying pan (skillet). Add the mustard seeds and cover the pan until they start to pop. Stir in the cumin seeds and coriander, turmeric and chilli. Stir until fragrant, about 1 minute.

2 Add the onion, garlic and (bell) pepper, and cook until soft, about 5 minutes, stirring frequently.

3 Add the okra to the pan and combine all the ingredients thoroughly.

4 Pour in the vegetable juice, bring to the boil and cook over a high heat for 5 minutes, stirring occasionally.

5 When most of the liquid has evaporated, check the seasoning.

6 Add the cream, bring to the boil again and continue to cook the mixture over a high heat for about 12 minutes until almost dry.

7 Sprinkle over the lemon juice and serve immediately.

Step *3*

Step *4*

Step *6*

Curried Okra

Okra, also known as bhindi and ladies' fingers, are a favourite Indian vegetable. They are now widely available.

SERVES 4

INGREDIENTS

500 g/1 lb fresh okra
4 tbsp vegetable ghee or oil
1 bunch spring onions (scallions),
trimmed and sliced
2 garlic cloves, crushed
5 cm/2 inch ginger root, chopped finely
1 tsp minced chilli (from a jar)
1½ tsp ground cumin
1 tsp ground coriander
1 tsp ground turmeric
250 g/7 oz can chopped tomatoes
150 ml/¼ pint/⅔ cup vegetable stock
1 tsp garam masala
salt and pepper
chopped fresh coriander (cilantro), to garnish

1 Wash the okra, trim off the stalks and pat dry. Heat the ghee or oil in a large pan, add the spring onions (scallions), garlic, ginger and chilli and fry gently for 1 minute, stirring frequently.

2 Stir in the spices and fry gently for 30 seconds, then add the tomatoes, stock and okra. Season with salt and pepper to taste and simmer for about 15 minutes, stirring and turning the mixture occasionally. The okra should be cooked but still a little crisp.

3 Sprinkle with the garam masala, taste and adjust the seasoning, if necessary. Garnish with the chopped coriander (cilantro) and serve hot.

Step *1*

Step *2*

Step *3*

Spicy Cauliflower

This is a perfectly delicious way to serve cauliflower. It is a dry dish so can be enjoyed as a salad or at a picnic, or as an accompaniment to a dhansak or korma.

SERVES 4

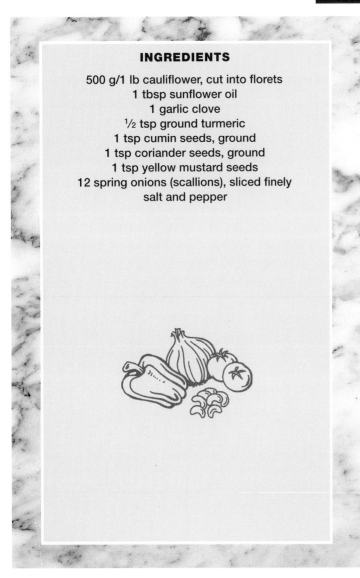

INGREDIENTS

500 g/1 lb cauliflower, cut into florets
1 tbsp sunflower oil
1 garlic clove
½ tsp ground turmeric
1 tsp cumin seeds, ground
1 tsp coriander seeds, ground
1 tsp yellow mustard seeds
12 spring onions (scallions), sliced finely
salt and pepper

1 Blanch the cauliflower in boiling water, drain and set aside. Cauliflower holds a lot of water, which tends to make it over-soft, so turn the florets upside-down at this stage and you will end up with a crisper result.

2 Heat the oil gently in a large, heavy frying pan (skillet) or wok. Add the garlic clove, turmeric, cumin, coriander and mustard seeds. Stir well and cover the pan.

3 When you hear the mustard seeds popping, add the spring onions (scallions) and stir. Cook for 2 minutes, stirring constantly, to soften them a little. Season to taste.

4 Add the cauliflower and stir for 3–4 minutes until coated completely with the spices and thoroughly heated.

5 Remove the garlic clove and serve immediately.

Step *1*

Step *2*

Step *4*

Spinach & Cauliflower Bhaji

This excellent vegetable dish goes well with most Indian food –
and it is simple and quick-cooking, too.

SERVES 4

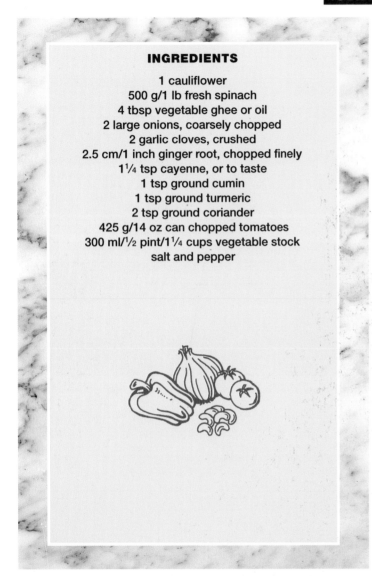

INGREDIENTS

1 cauliflower
500 g/1 lb fresh spinach
4 tbsp vegetable ghee or oil
2 large onions, coarsely chopped
2 garlic cloves, crushed
2.5 cm/1 inch ginger root, chopped finely
1¼ tsp cayenne, or to taste
1 tsp ground cumin
1 tsp ground turmeric
2 tsp ground coriander
425 g/14 oz can chopped tomatoes
300 ml/½ pint/1¼ cups vegetable stock
salt and pepper

1 Divide the cauliflower into small florets, discarding the hard central stalk. Trim the stalks from spinach leaves. Heat the ghee or oil in a large saucepan, add the onions and cauliflower florets, and fry the vegetables gently for about 3 minutes, stirring frequently.

2 Add the garlic, ginger and spices and cook gently for 1 minute. Stir in the tomatoes and the stock, and season with salt and pepper. Bring to the boil, cover, reduce the heat and simmer gently for 8 minutes.

3 Add the spinach to the pan, stirring and turning to wilt the leaves. Cover and simmer gently for about 8–10 minutes, stirring frequently until the spinach has wilted and the cauliflower is tender. Serve hot.

Step *1*

Step *2*

Step *3*

Kashmiri Spinach

This is an imaginative way to serve spinach, which adds a little zip to it.
It is a very simple dish, which will complement almost any curry.

SERVES 4

INGREDIENTS

500g/1lb spinach (Swiss chard or
baby leaf spinach may be substituted)
2 tbsp mustard oil
¼ tsp garam masala
1 tsp yellow mustard seeds
2 spring onions (scallions), sliced

1 Remove the tough stalks from the spinach.

2 Heat the mustard oil in a wok or large heavy frying pan (skillet) until it smokes. Add the garam masala and mustard seeds. Cover the pan quickly – you will hear the mustard seeds popping inside.

3 When the popping has ceased, remove the cover, add the spring onions (scallions) and stir in the spinach until wilted.

4 Continue cooking the spinach, uncovered, over a medium heat for 10–15 minutes, until most of the water has evaporated. If using frozen spinach, it will not need as much cooking – cook it until most of the water has evaporated.

5 Remove the spinach and spring onions (scallions) with a perforated spoon in order to drain off any remaining liquid. This dish is more pleasant to eat when it is served as dry as possible. Serve immediately while it is piping hot.

Step *1*

Step *3*

Step *5*

Spicy Indian-Style Potatoes

Potatoes cooked this way are so delicious, yet quick and simple to prepare.
Cut the potatoes into similar-sized pieces to make sure they cook evenly.

SERVES 4

INGREDIENTS

750 g/1½ lb potatoes
60 g/2 oz/¼ cup ghee or butter
2 tbsp vegetable oil
1 tsp ground turmeric
1 large onion, quartered and sliced
2–3 garlic cloves, crushed
5 cm/2 inch piece ginger root, chopped finely
1½ tsp cumin seeds
¼–½ tsp cayenne
2 tsp lemon juice
1 tbsp shredded mint leaves
salt
mint sprigs, to garnish

1 Peel the potatoes and cut into 2–2.5 cm/¾–1 inch cubes. Cook in a pan of boiling, salted water for 6–8 minutes or until knife-tip tender (do not overcook). Drain well, return to the pan and shake dry over a moderate heat for a few moments.

2 Heat the ghee or butter and oil in a large frying pan over medium heat. Stir in the turmeric, then add the onion and the potatoes and fry for 4–5 minutes or until the mixture is beginning to brown, stirring and turning the vegetables frequently.

3 Stir in the garlic, ginger, cumin seeds, cayenne and salt to taste. Fry over gentle heat for 1 minute, stirring all the time.

4 Transfer the potatoes to a warm serving dish. Add the lemon juice to the juices in the pan and spoon the mixture over the potatoes. Sprinkle with the shredded mint leaves, garnish with mint sprigs and serve hot.

Step *1*

Step *2*

Step *3*

Fried Spiced Potatoes

Deliciously good and a super accompaniment to almost any main course dish, though rather high in calories!

SERVES 4–6

INGREDIENTS

2 onions, chopped coarsely
5 cm/2 inch ginger root, chopped
2 garlic cloves
2–3 tbsp mild or medium curry paste
4 tbsp water
750 g/1½ lb new potatoes
vegetable oil, for deep frying
3 tbsp vegetable ghee or oil
150 ml/¼ pint/⅔ cup strained thick yogurt
150 ml/¼ pint/⅔ cup double (heavy) cream
3 tbsp chopped fresh mint
salt and pepper
½ bunch spring onions (scallions),
trimmed and chopped, to garnish

1 Place the onions, ginger, garlic, curry paste and water in a blender or food processor and process until smooth, scraping down the sides of machine and blending again, if necessary.

2 Cut the potatoes into quarters – the pieces need to be about 2.5 cm/1 inch in size – and pat dry with paper towels. Heat the oil in a deep-fat fryer to 180°C/350°F and fry the potatoes, in batches, for about 5 minutes or until golden brown, turning frequently. Remove from the pan and drain on paper towels.

3 Heat the ghee or oil in a large frying pan, add the onion mixture and fry gently for 2 minutes, stirring all the time. Add the yogurt, cream and 2 tablespoons of the mint and mix well.

4 Add the fried potatoes and stir until coated in the sauce. Cook for a further 5–7 minutes or until heated through and the sauce has thickened, stirring frequently. Season with salt and pepper to taste and sprinkle with the remaining mint and sliced spring onions (scallions). Serve immediately.

Step *1*

Step *2*

Step *4*

Curried Roast Potatoes

This Indian-inspired dish would fit easily into any Western menu, or how about serving with a curry in place of the more traditional rice?

SERVES 4

INGREDIENTS

2 tsp cumin seeds
2 tsp coriander seeds
90 g/3 oz/⅓ cup salted butter
1 tsp ground turmeric
1 tsp black mustard seeds
2 garlic cloves, crushed
2 dried red chillies
750 g/1½ lb baby new potatoes

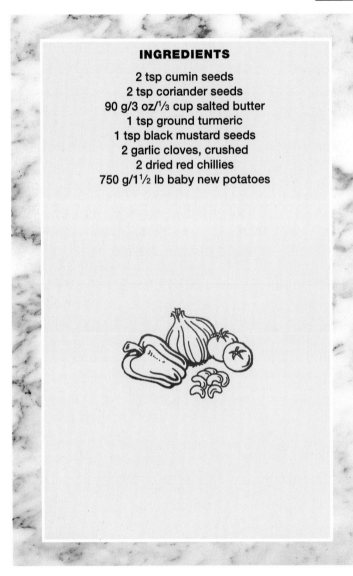

1 Grind the cumin and coriander seeds together with a pestle and mortar or spice grinder. Grinding them fresh like this captures all of the flavour before it has a chance to dry out.

2 Melt the butter gently in a roasting tin (pan) and add the turmeric, mustard seeds, garlic and chillies and the ground cumin and coriander seeds. Stir well to combine evenly. Place in a preheated oven, 200°C/400°F/Gas Mark 6, for 5 minutes.

3 Remove the tin (pan) from the oven – the spices should be very fragrant at this stage – and add the potatoes. Stir well so that the butter and spice mix coats the potatoes completely.

4 Put back in the preheated oven and bake for 20–25 minutes. Stir occasionally to ensure that the potatoes are coated evenly. Test the potatoes with a skewer – if they drop off the end of the skewer when lifted, they are done. Serve immediately.

Step *1*

Step *2*

Step *4*

Potato Fritters with Relish

These are incredibly simple to make and sure to be popular served as a tempting snack or as an accompaniment to almost any Indian main course dish.

MAKES 8

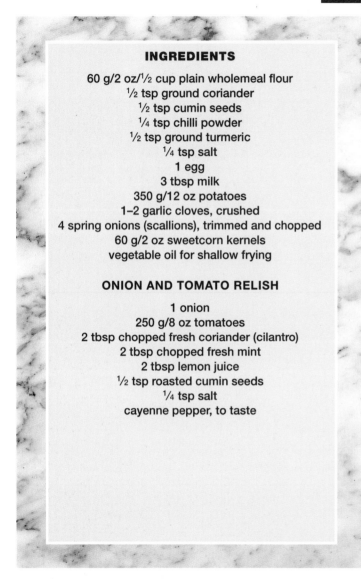

INGREDIENTS

60 g/2 oz/½ cup plain wholemeal flour
½ tsp ground coriander
½ tsp cumin seeds
¼ tsp chilli powder
½ tsp ground turmeric
¼ tsp salt
1 egg
3 tbsp milk
350 g/12 oz potatoes
1–2 garlic cloves, crushed
4 spring onions (scallions), trimmed and chopped
60 g/2 oz sweetcorn kernels
vegetable oil for shallow frying

ONION AND TOMATO RELISH

1 onion
250 g/8 oz tomatoes
2 tbsp chopped fresh coriander (cilantro)
2 tbsp chopped fresh mint
2 tbsp lemon juice
½ tsp roasted cumin seeds
¼ tsp salt
cayenne pepper, to taste

1 First make the relish. Cut the onion and tomatoes into small dice and place in a bowl with the remaining ingredients. Mix well and leave to stand for at least 15 minutes before serving to allow the flavours to blend.

2 Place the flour in a bowl, stir in the spices and salt and make a well in the centre. Add the egg and milk and mix to form a fairly thick batter.

3 Coarsely grate the potatoes, place in a sieve and rinse well under cold running water. Drain and squeeze dry, then stir into the batter with the garlic, spring onions (scallions)and corn.

4 Heat about 5 mm/¼ inch oil in a large frying pan and add a few tablespoonfuls of the mixture at a time, flattening each one to form a thin cake. Fry gently for 2–3 minutes or until golden brown and cooked through, turning frequently.

5 Drain on paper towels and keep hot while frying the remaining mixture in the same way. Serve hot with onion and tomato relish.

Step *1*

Step *2*

Step *5*

Aloo Chat

Aloo Chat (chat means salad) is one of a variety of Indian foods served at any time of the day, to satisfy and stimulate the appetite.

SERVES 4

INGREDIENTS

125 g/4 oz/generous ½ cup chick-peas
(garbanzo beans), soaked overnight in
cold water and drained
1 dried red chilli
500 g/1 lb waxy potatoes,
boiled in their skins and peeled
1 tsp cumin seeds
1 tsp black peppercorns
2 tsp salt
½ tsp dried mint
½ tsp chilli powder
½ tsp ground ginger
2 tsp mango powder
120 ml/4 fl oz/½ cup natural yogurt
oil for deep frying
4 poppadoms
Cucumber Raita (page 234), to serve

1 Boil the chick-peas (garbanzo beans) with the chilli in plenty of water for about 1 hour until tender. Drain.

2 Cut the potatoes into 2.5 cm/1 inch dice and mix with the chick-peas (garbanzo beans) while they are still warm. Set aside.

3 Grind together the cumin, peppercorns and salt in a spice grinder or with a pestle and mortar. Stir in the mint, chilli powder, ginger and mango powder.

4 Put a small dry saucepan or frying pan (skillet) over a low heat and add the spice mix. Stir until fragrant then immediately remove from the heat.

5 Stir half of the spice mix into the chick-peas (garbanzo beans) and potatoes, and stir the rest into the yogurt.

6 Cook the poppadoms according to the pack instructions. Drain on plenty of paper towels. Break into bite-size pieces and stir into the potatoes and chick-peas (garbanzo beans). Spoon over the spiced yogurt and serve with the cucumber raita.

Step *1*

Step *2*

Step *4*

Muttar Paneer

Paneer is a delicious fresh, soft cheese frequently used in Indian cooking. It is easily made at home, but remember to make it the day before required.

SERVES 6

INGREDIENTS

150 ml/¼ pint/⅔ cup vegetable oil
2 onions, chopped
2 garlic cloves, crushed
2.5 cm/1 inch ginger root, chopped finely
1 tsp garam masala
1 tsp ground turmeric
1 tsp chilli powder
500 g/1 lb frozen peas
250 g/7 oz can chopped tomatoes
125 ml/4 fl oz/½ cup vegetable stock
salt and pepper
2 tbsp chopped fresh coriander
(cilantro), to garnish

PANEER

2.5 litres/4 pints/10 cups milk
5 tbsp lemon juice
1 garlic clove, crushed (optional)
1 tbsp chopped fresh coriander (cilantro) (optional)

1 To make the paneer, bring the milk to a rolling boil in a large saucepan. Remove from the heat and stir in the lemon juice. Return to the heat for about 1 minute until the curds and whey separate. Remove from the heat. Line a colander with double thickness muslin and pour the mixture through the muslin, adding the garlic and coriander, if using. Squeeze all the liquid from the curds and leave to drain.

2 Transfer to a dish, cover with a plate and weights and leave overnight in the refrigerator.

3 Cut the pressed paneer into small cubes. Heat the oil in a large frying pan, add the paneer cubes and fry until golden on all sides. Remove from the pan and drain on paper towels.

4 Pour off some of the oil, leaving about 4 tablespoons in the pan. Add the onions, garlic and ginger and fry gently for about 5 minutes, stirring frequently. Stir in the spices and fry gently for 2 minutes. Add the peas, tomatoes and stock, and season with salt and pepper. Cover and simmer for 10 minutes, stirring occasionally, until the onion is tender.

5 Add the fried paneer cubes and cook for a further 5 minutes. Taste and adjust the seasoning, if necessary. Sprinkle with the coriander (cilantro) and serve at once.

Step *1*

Step *4*

Step *5*

Palak Paneer

*Paneer, curd cheese, figures widely on Indian menus. It is combined with
all sorts of ingredients, but most popularly with spinach and vegetables.*

SERVES 4–6

INGREDIENTS

2 tbsp ghee
1 onion, sliced
1 garlic clove, crushed
1 dried red chilli
1 tsp ground turmeric
500 g/1 lb waxy potatoes,
cut into 2.5 cm/1 inch cubes
425 g/14 oz can tomatoes, drained
150 ml/¼ pint/⅔ cup water
250 g/8 oz/6 cups fresh spinach
500 g/1 lb/2 cups Paneer
(page 158), cut into 2.5 cm/1 inch cubes
1 tsp garam masala
1 tbsp chopped fresh coriander (cilantro)
1 tbsp chopped fresh parsley
salt and pepper
naan bread, to serve

1 Heat the ghee in a saucepan, add the onion and cook over a low heat for 10 minutes until very soft. Add the garlic and chilli and cook for a further 5 minutes.

2 Add the turmeric, salt, potatoes, tomatoes and water and bring to the boil.

3 Simmer for 10 –15 minutes until the potatoes are cooked.

4 Stir in the spinach, cheese cubes, garam masala, coriander (cilantro) and parsley and season to taste.

5 Simmer for a further 5 minutes and season well. Serve with naan bread.

Step *1*

Step *2*

Step *4*

RICE DISHES

Rice is a staple ingredient in India and has been used in cooking for thousands of years. It is the first food that a new Indian bride offers her husband; it is also the first food offered to a new-born child.

Despite the mystique and ritual surrounding the cooking of rice, it is one of the most straightforward grains to prepare. A bowl of fluffy rice, delicately flavoured with mild spices, is served at virtually every main meal in India, and acts as a filling base and a foil for the richer, spicier dishes.

The stunning mountain ranges that are the Himalayas provide the crystal-clear mineral water that is used to grow basmati rice. For basmati rice to be classified as such, it must be grown in the foothills of the Himalayas. However, it is such a desirable commodity in the world market that due to 'creative' sales techniques, more 'basmati' rice is sold each year than is harvested! Described as the 'prince of rice', basmati rice has a greater fragrance and a nuttier taste than ordinary long-grain rice, and it has a longer, more slender grain.

Aromatic Pilau

*This rice dish forms the perfect accompaniment to most main courses. It can be
prepared ahead of time and reheated in the microwave oven just before serving.*

SERVES 4–5

INGREDIENTS

250 g/8 oz/1¼ cups basmati rice
2 tbsp ghee or vegetable oil
1 onion, chopped
3 cardamom pods, crushed
3 black peppercorns
3 cloves
1 tsp cumin seeds
½ cinnamon stick or piece of cassia bark
½ tsp ground turmeric
600 ml/1 pint/2½ cups boiling water or stock
60 g/2 oz/⅓ cup seedless raisins or
sultanas (golden raisins)
60 g/2 oz frozen peas
30 g/1 oz/¼ cup flaked (slivered) almonds, toasted
salt and pepper
crisp fried onion rings (optional), to garnish

1 Place the rice in a sieve and wash well under cold
running water until the water runs clear. Drain well.

2 Heat the oil in a large saucepan, add the onion and
spices and fry gently for 1 minute, stirring all the
time. Stir in the rice and mix well until coated in the
spiced oil, then add the boiling water or stock, and season
with salt and pepper to taste.

3 Bring to the boil, stir well, then cover, reduce the heat
and cook gently for 15 minutes without uncovering.
Add the raisins and peas, re-cover and leave to stand for
15 minutes.

4 Uncover, fluff up with a fork and stir the toasted
flaked almonds into the mixture. Serve hot, garnished
with crisp fried onion rings, if liked.

Step *2*

Step *3*

Step *4*

Spiced Basmati Pilau

Omit the broccoli and mushrooms from this recipe if you require only a simple spiced pilau. Remove the whole spices before serving.

SERVES 6

INGREDIENTS

500 g/1 lb/2½ cups basmati rice
175 g/6 oz broccoli, trimmed
6 tbsp vegetable oil
2 large onions, chopped
250 g/8 oz mushrooms, wiped and sliced
2 garlic cloves, crushed
6 cardamom pods, split
6 whole cloves
8 black peppercorns
1 cinnamon stick or piece of cassia bark
1 tsp ground turmeric
1.25 litres/2 pints/5 cups boiling
vegetable stock or water
60 g/2 oz/⅓ cup seedless raisins
60 g/2 oz/½ cup unsalted pistachios, coarsely
chopped
salt and pepper

1 Place the rice in a sieve and wash well under cold running water until the water runs clear. Drain. Trim off most of the broccoli stalk and cut into small florets, then quarter the stalk lengthways and cut diagonally into 1 cm/½ inch pieces.

2 Heat the oil in a large saucepan, add the onions and broccoli stalks and cook gently for 3 minutes, stirring frequently. Add the mushrooms, rice, garlic and spices and cook gently for 1 minute, stirring frequently until the rice is coated in spiced oil.

3 Add the boiling stock and season with salt and pepper. Stir in the broccoli florets and bring the mixture back to the boil. Cover, reduce the heat and cook gently for 15 minutes without uncovering.

4 Remove from the heat and leave to stand for 5 minutes without uncovering. Add the raisins and pistachios and gently fork through to fluff up the grains. Serve hot.

Step *1*

Step *3*

Step *4*

Prawn (Shrimp) Pilau

This is an Arabian-inspired creation, reminiscent of the spice trade of Sri Lanka. Serve it at family meals, sophisticated dinner parties and buffets.

SERVES 4–6

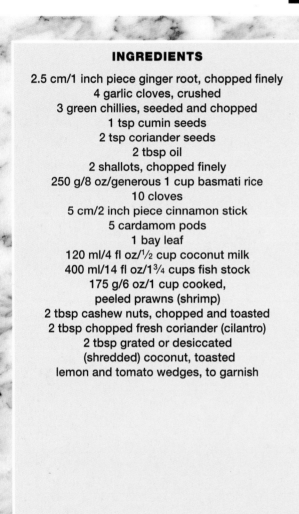

INGREDIENTS

2.5 cm/1 inch piece ginger root, chopped finely
4 garlic cloves, crushed
3 green chillies, seeded and chopped
1 tsp cumin seeds
2 tsp coriander seeds
2 tbsp oil
2 shallots, chopped finely
250 g/8 oz/generous 1 cup basmati rice
10 cloves
5 cm/2 inch piece cinnamon stick
5 cardamom pods
1 bay leaf
120 ml/4 fl oz/½ cup coconut milk
400 ml/14 fl oz/1¾ cups fish stock
175 g/6 oz/1 cup cooked,
peeled prawns (shrimp)
2 tbsp cashew nuts, chopped and toasted
2 tbsp chopped fresh coriander (cilantro)
2 tbsp grated or desiccated
(shredded) coconut, toasted
lemon and tomato wedges, to garnish

1 Grind together the ginger, garlic and green chillies in a coffee grinder or pestle and mortar.

2 Toast the cumin and coriander seeds and then grind them also.

3 Heat the oil in a wok or large frying pan (skillet). Add the shallots and cook over a medium heat until soft, about 5 minutes. Add the garlic mixture and stir until fragrant, about 1 minute. Add the cumin and coriander. Add the rice and stir until translucent.

4 Put the cloves, cinnamon, cardamom and bay leaf into a piece of muslin (cheesecloth). This is not essential but it makes them easier to remove at the end. Add the bag of spices to the pan.

5 Stir in the coconut milk and fish stock. Bring to the boil, stir once and simmer for 15–18 minutes, or until all the liquid is absorbed.

6 Add the prawns (shrimp), cashew nuts and coriander (cilantro). Cover with a close-fitting lid or a piece of foil, reduce the heat to the lowest setting and leave undisturbed for 10 minutes.

7 Discard the muslin (cheesecloth) bag of spices. Transfer the pilau to a serving dish and fork through lightly. Sprinkle over the toasted coconut and garnish with the lemon and tomato.

Step *2*

Step *4*

Step *6*

Hyderabad Rice Pilau

This is a wonderfully colourful pilau, full of spice and flavour and aromatic ingredients, from exotic okra to saffron and hot cayenne.

SERVES 6

INGREDIENTS

3 tbsp sunflower oil
1 onion, sliced finely
3 shallots, chopped finely
1 garlic clove, crushed
1 tsp grated ginger root
425 g/14 oz/2 cups basmati rice
½ tsp cayenne
250 g/8 oz/2 cups okra, trimmed
1 litre/1¾ pints/4 cups chicken stock
1 tsp saffron, crushed lightly
rind of ½ orange, without pith
60 g/2 oz/⅓ cup sultanas (golden raisins)
1 tbsp lemon juice

TO GARNISH

30 g/1 oz flaked (slivered) almonds, toasted
1 tsp chopped fresh mint
1 tsp chopped fresh coriander (cilantro)

1 Heat the oil in a wok or large frying pan (skillet) until quite hot. Fry the onions until golden brown, then remove and drain on paper towels. Do not cook them all at once, as they won't be crispy.

2 Reduce the heat. Cook the shallots in the remaining oil until soft, about 5 minutes. Add the garlic and ginger, and stir. Stir in the rice, cayenne and okra.

3 Pour in the chicken stock, and add the saffron and orange rind. Bring to the boil and simmer over a moderate heat for 15 minutes.

4 Add the sultanas (golden raisins) at the end of this time and stir in the lemon juice.

5 Remove the piece of orange rind if you prefer, then transfer to a serving dish and garnish with the fried onion, toasted almonds, mint and coriander (cilantro).

Step *1*

Step *3*

Step *4*

Aromatic Basmati Rice & Saffron Rice

*For the best results when cooking basmati rice, rinse the raw rice under
the tap and then soak in cold water for 30 minutes.*

SERVES 4

INGREDIENTS

AROMATIC BASMATI RICE

1 tbsp oil
1 cinnamon stick
2 bay leaves
4 green cardamom pods
4 black peppercorns
250 g/8 oz/1 cup basmati rice,
washed and soaked
1 tsp salt

SPICY SAFFRON RICE

60 g/2 oz/¼ cup butter or ghee
1 onion, chopped
½ tsp saffron strands
1 tsp cumin seeds
250 g/8 oz/1 cup basmati rice,
washed and soaked
1 tsp salt
90 g/3 oz/⅔ cup split almonds,
¾ cut in slivers and toasted

1 To make the aromatic rice, heat the oil in a heavy-based saucepan and fry the cinnamon, bay leaves, cardamom pods and black peppercorns for 30 seconds.

2 Add the rice, salt and enough water to cover the rice by 2.5 cm/1 inch. Cover with a tight-fitting lid, bring to the boil and simmer for 20 minutes or until all the water has been absorbed and the rice is tender.

3 To make the saffron rice, heat the butter or ghee in a heavy- based saucepan, add the onion and stir-fry. Add the saffron strands and cumin seeds and fry for 30 seconds.

4 Add the rice and fry for 2 minutes until it has absorbed the oil and the saffron colour.

5 Add the salt and enough water to cover the rice by 2.5 cm/1 inch. Cover with a tight-fitting lid and simmer for 20 minutes until all the water has been absorbed and the rice is tender. Stir in the almonds.

Step *1*

Step *2*

Step *4*

Brown Rice with Fruit & Nuts

Here is a tasty and filling rice dish that is nice and spicy and includes fruits for a refreshing flavour and toasted nuts for an interesting crunchy texture.

SERVES 4-6

INGREDIENTS

4 tbsp vegetable ghee or oil
1 large onion, chopped
2 garlic cloves, crushed
2.5 cm/1 in ginger root,
chopped finely
1 tsp chilli powder
1 tsp cumin seeds
1 tbsp mild or medium
curry powder or paste
300 g/10 oz/1½ cups brown rice
900 ml/1½ pints/3½ cups boiling
vegetable stock
425 g/14 oz can chopped tomatoes
175 g/6 oz ready-soaked dried apricots
or peaches, cut into slivers
1 red (bell) pepper, cored,
seeded and diced
90 g/3 oz frozen peas
1–2 small, slightly green bananas
60–90g /2–3 oz/ ⅓–½ cup toasted mixed nuts
salt and pepper
coriander (cilantro) sprigs, to garnish

1 Heat the ghee or oil in a large saucepan, add the onion and fry gently for 3 minutes. Stir in the garlic, ginger, spices and rice. Cook gently for 2 minutes, stirring all the time until the rice is coated in the spiced oil.

2 Pour in the boiling stock. Add the tomatoes and season with salt and pepper to taste. Bring to the boil, then reduce the heat, cover and simmer gently for 40 minutes or until the rice is almost cooked and most of the liquid is absorbed.

3 Add the apricots or peaches, red (bell) pepper and peas. Cover and continue cooking for 10 minutes. Remove from the heat and allow to stand for 5 minutes without uncovering.

4 Peel and slice the bananas. Uncover the rice mixture and toss with a fork to mix. Add the toasted nuts and sliced banana and toss lightly. Transfer to a warm serving platter and garnish with coriander (cilantro) sprigs. Serve hot.

Step *1*

Step *3*

Step *4*

Prawn (Shrimp) Biryani

Like Lamb Biryani (page 180), this dish is usually served on special occasions because it needs close attention during cooking.

SERVES 6–8

INGREDIENTS

250 g/8 oz/generous 1 cup basmati rice,
rinsed and drained
1 tsp saffron strands
50 ml/2 fl oz/4 tbsp tepid water
2 shallots, chopped coarsely
3 garlic cloves, crushed
1 tsp chopped ginger root
2 tsp coriander seeds
½ tsp black peppercorns
2 cloves
2 green cardamom pods
2.5 cm/1 inch piece cinnamon stick
1 tsp ground turmeric
1 fresh green chilli, chopped
½ tsp salt
2 tbsp ghee
1 tsp black mustard seeds
500 g/1 lb uncooked tiger prawns (shrimp)
in their shells, or 425 g/14 oz peeled
uncooked tiger prawns (shrimp), or cooked
and peeled Atlantic prawns (shrimp)
300 ml/½ pint/1¼ cups coconut milk
300 ml/½ pint/1¼ cups natural yogurt
1 tbsp sultanas (golden raisins)

TO GARNISH

3 tbsp flaked (slivered) almonds, toasted
1 spring onion (scallion), sliced

1 Soak the rice in cold water for 30 minutes. Combine the saffron with the water and soak for 10 minutes.

2 Put the shallots, garlic, ginger, coriander, peppercorns, cloves, cardamom, cinnamon, turmeric, chilli and salt in a spice grinder or pestle and mortar and grind to a paste.

3 Heat the ghee in a large saucepan and add the mustard seeds. When they start to pop, add the prawns (shrimp) and stir over a high heat for 1 minute. Stir in the spice mix.

4 Add the coconut milk and yogurt, and simmer for 20 minutes.

5 Meanwhile, bring a large saucepan of salted water to the boil. Drain the rice and slowly add to the pan. Boil for 12 minutes. Drain. Carefully pile the rice on the prawns. Spoon over the sultanas (golden raisins) and trickle the saffron solution in lines over the rice.

6 Cover the pan with a clean tea towel or dish towel and put the lid on tightly. Remove the pan from heat and leave to stand for 5 minutes to infuse. Serve, garnished with the toasted almonds and spring onion (scallion).

Step *3*

Step *4*

Step *6*

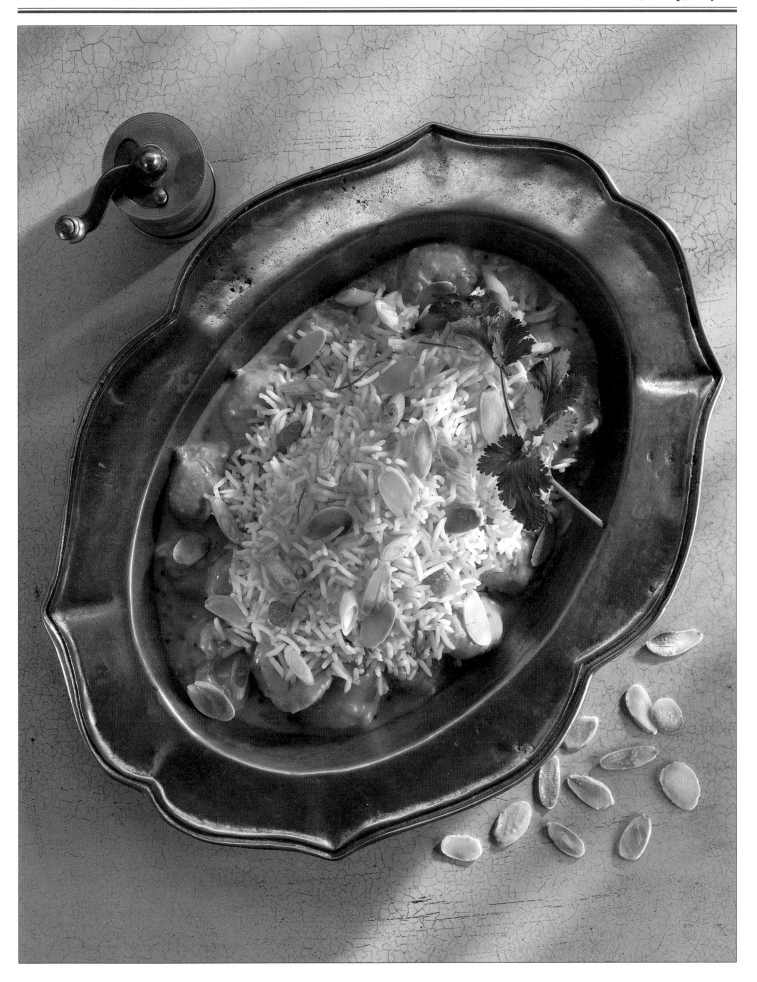

Lentil & Vegetable Biryani

*A delicious mix of vegetables, basmati rice and lentils produces a
wholesome and nutritious dish.*

SERVES 6

INGREDIENTS

125 g/4 oz/²⁄₃ cup brown or green lentils
4 tbsp vegetable ghee or oil
2 onions, quartered and sliced
2 garlic cloves, crushed
2.5 cm/1 inch ginger root, chopped finely
1 tsp ground turmeric
½ tsp chilli powder
1 tsp ground coriander
2 tsp ground cumin
3 tomatoes, skinned and chopped
1 aubergine (eggplant), trimmed and
cut in 1 cm/½ inch pieces
1.75 litres/2½ pints/6¼ cups
boiling vegetable stock
1 red or green (bell) pepper,
seeded and diced
350 g/12 oz/1¾ cups basmati rice,
rinsed, drained and soaked in
cold water for 30 minutes
125 g/4 oz/1 cup French (green) beans,
topped, tailed and halved
250 g/8 oz/1⅓ cups cauliflower florets
125 g/4 oz/1½ cups mushrooms,
wiped and sliced
60 g/2 oz/½ cup unsalted cashews

TO GARNISH

3 hard-boiled eggs, shelled
coriander (cilantro) sprigs

1 Rinse the lentils under cold running water and drain. Heat the ghee or oil in a saucepan, add the onions and fry gently for 2 minutes. Stir in the garlic, ginger and spices and fry gently for 1 minute, stirring frequently.

2 Stir in the lentils, tomatoes, aubergine (eggplant) and 600 ml/1 pint/2½ cups of the stock. Cover and simmer gently for 20 minutes. Add the red or green (bell) pepper and cook for a further 10 minutes or until the lentils are tender and all the liquid has been absorbed.

3 Drain the rice and put in another pan with the remaining stock. Bring to the boil, add the French (green) beans, cauliflower and mushrooms, then cover and cook gently for 15 minutes or until rice and vegetables are tender. Remove from the heat and leave to stand for 10 minutes, covered.

4 Add the lentil mixture and the cashews to the cooked rice and mix lightly. Pile on to a warm serving platter and garnish with wedges of hard-boiled egg and coriander (cilantro) sprigs. Serve hot.

Step *2*

Step *3*

Step *4*

Lamb Biryani

In India this elaborate, beautifully coloured dish is usually served at parties and on festive occasions. This version can be made on any day, festive or not.

SERVES 4

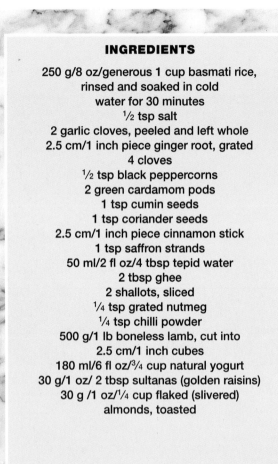

INGREDIENTS

250 g/8 oz/generous 1 cup basmati rice,
rinsed and soaked in cold
water for 30 minutes
½ tsp salt
2 garlic cloves, peeled and left whole
2.5 cm/1 inch piece ginger root, grated
4 cloves
½ tsp black peppercorns
2 green cardamom pods
1 tsp cumin seeds
1 tsp coriander seeds
2.5 cm/1 inch piece cinnamon stick
1 tsp saffron strands
50 ml/2 fl oz/4 tbsp tepid water
2 tbsp ghee
2 shallots, sliced
¼ tsp grated nutmeg
¼ tsp chilli powder
500 g/1 lb boneless lamb, cut into
2.5 cm/1 inch cubes
180 ml/6 fl oz/¾ cup natural yogurt
30 g/1 oz/ 2 tbsp sultanas (golden raisins)
30 g /1 oz/¼ cup flaked (slivered)
almonds, toasted

1 Bring a large saucepan of salted water to the boil. Add the rice and boil for 6 minutes. Drain and set aside.

2 Grind together the garlic, ginger, cloves, peppercorns, cardamom pods, cumin, coriander and cinnamon.

3 Combine the saffron and water, and set aside. Heat the ghee in a large saucepan and add the shallots. Fry until golden brown then add the ground spice mix, nutmeg and chilli powder. Stir for 1 minute and add the lamb. Cook until evenly browned.

4 Add the yogurt, stirring constantly, then the sultanas (golden raisins) and bring to a simmer. Cook for 40 minutes, stirring occasionally.

5 Carefully pile the rice on the sauce, in a pyramid shape. Trickle the saffron solution over the rice in lines. Cover the pan with a clean tea towel and put on the lid. Reduce the heat to low and cook for 10 minutes. Remove the lid and tea towel, and quickly make 3 holes in the rice with a wooden spoon handle, to the level of the sauce, but not touching it. Replace the tea towel and the lid and leave to stand for 5 minutes.

6 Remove the lid and tea towel, lightly fork the rice and serve, sprinkled with the toasted almonds.

Step *1*

Step *3*

Step *5*

Kitchouri

*This is the dish from which kedgeree evolved. The English colonists
adopted it, adding preserved fish, to make the version we know today.*

SERVES 4

INGREDIENTS

2 tbsp ghee or butter
1 red onion, chopped finely
1 garlic clove, crushed
½ celery stick, chopped finely
1 tsp turmeric
½ tsp garam masala
1 green chilli, seeded and chopped finely
½ tsp cumin seeds
1 tbsp chopped fresh coriander (cilantro)
125 g/4 oz/generous ½ cup basmati rice,
rinsed and soaked in cold
water for 30 minutes
125 g/4 oz/½ cup green lentils
300 ml/½ pint/1¼ cups vegetable juice
600 ml/1 pint/2½ cups vegetable stock

1 Melt the ghee in a large saucepan. Add the onion, garlic and celery, and cook until soft, about 5 minutes.

2 Add the turmeric, garam masala, chilli, cumin seeds and coriander (cilantro). Stir until fragrant over a moderate heat, about 1 minute.

3 Add the rice and lentils. Stir until the rice is translucent, about 1 minute.

4 Pour the vegetable juice and vegetable stock into the saucepan, and bring to the boil. Cover and simmer over a low heat for about 20 minutes, stirring occasionally, or until the lentils are tender.

5 Transfer to a warmed serving dish and serve hot.

Step *1*

Step *2*

Step *4*

Coconut Rice

A delicious rice dish flavoured with coconut and lemon. For a luxurious touch you can fork in a few shelled, chopped pistachios at the final stage.

SERVES 4–5

INGREDIENTS

250 g/8 oz/1¼ cups basmati rice
3 tbsp ghee or vegetable oil
1 onion, chopped
2 garlic cloves, crushed
2.5 cm/1 inch piece ginger root,
chopped finely
½ cinnamon stick or piece of cassia bark
2 carrots, grated
600 ml/1 pint/2½ cups boiling water or stock
30 g/1 oz creamed coconut, chopped finely
finely grated rind of ½ lemon or 1 lime
1 tbsp chopped fresh coriander (cilantro)
1 bunch spring onions (scallions),
trimmed and sliced
salt and pepper

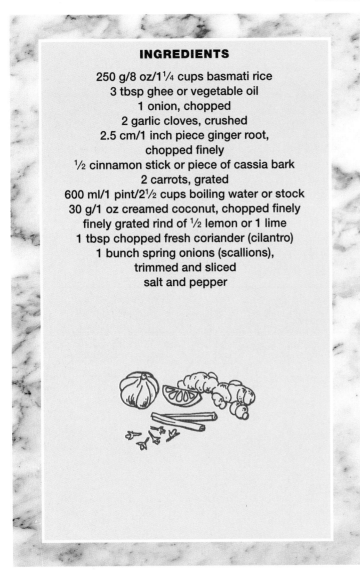

1 Place the rice in a sieve and wash well under cold running water until the water runs clear. Drain well, then soak in cold water for 30 minutes and drain again.

2 Heat the ghee or oil in a large saucepan, add the onion, garlic, ginger and cinnamon and fry gently for 1 minute. Stir in the rice and grated carrots and mix until well coated with the oil.

3 Stir in the water or stock and season with salt and pepper. Bring to the boil, cover, reduce the heat and simmer gently for 15 minutes without taking off the lid.

4 Add the creamed coconut, lemon rind, chopped coriander (cilantro) and spring onions (scallions), fork through and serve immediately.

Step *2*

Step *3*

Step *4*

Saffron Rice

This is the classic way to serve rice, paired with saffron, so that each brings out the best in the other.

SERVES 8

INGREDIENTS

12 saffron threads, crushed lightly
2 tbsp warm water
400 ml/14 fl oz/1¾ cups water
250 g/8 oz/generous 1 cup basmati rice,
rinsed and soaked in cold
water for 30 minutes
1 tbsp toasted, flaked (slivered) almonds

1 Put the saffron threads into a bowl with the warm water and leave for 10 minutes. They need to be crushed before soaking to ensure that the maximum flavour and colour is extracted at this stage.

2 Put the water and rice into a medium saucepan and set it over the heat to boil. Stir in the saffron solution.

3 Bring back to a gentle boil, stir again and let the rice simmer, uncovered, for about 10 minutes, until all the water has been absorbed.

4 Cover tightly, reduce the heat to a very low heat and leave for 10 minutes. Do not remove the lid. This method ensures that the grains separate and that the rice is not soggy.

5 Remove from the heat and transfer to a serving dish. Fork through the rice gently and sprinkle on the toasted almonds before serving.

Step *1*

Step *2*

Step *5*

PULSE DISHES

It is true, in the south of India at least, that Hindus are predominately vegetarian. In the north they are influenced by their Muslim and Persian neighbours, and more of the northern Hindus eat meat. But wherever you are in India, the meat is not always the tender, succulent product that we have come to expect in the West. This protein source often has to be supplemented, and there is a huge range and variety of pulses – dals – available.

Many Indians – and for that matter visitors to India – do survive on rice and dal or some sort of lentil stew for days or even weeks. Although it seems an unvaried diet, it is nourishing and quite satisfying.

Thali is one of the ways in which rice and dal are eaten; it takes its name from the tray on which the dish is served – a round metal tray holding six or seven small metal dishes (katoris) around the edge, leaving room for a large pile of rice in the middle. This southern Indian dish will usually have two or three dals, a curried vegetable, relishes, chutney and a few poppadoms, and they are especially tasty. A thali is standard Indian Railway fare, appearing magically fresh and hot as it is served to hundreds of passengers en route.

Yellow Split Pea Casserole

If ever there was a winter warmer, this is it – an intensely satisfying dish,
ideal for serving with a lightweight main dish such as pilau or biryani.

SERVES 6

INGREDIENTS

2 tbsp ghee
1 tsp black mustard seeds
1 onion, chopped finely
2 garlic cloves, crushed
1 carrot, grated
2.5 cm/1 inch piece ginger root, grated
1 green chilli, seeded and chopped finely
1 tbsp tomato purée (paste)
250 g/8 oz/1 cup yellow split peas,
soaked in water for 2 hours and drained
425 g/14 oz can chopped tomatoes
500 ml/16 fl oz/2 cups vegetable stock
250 g/8 oz/1½ cups pumpkin, cubed
250 g/8 oz cauliflower, cut into florets
2 tbsp oil
1 large aubergine (eggplant), cubed
1 tbsp chopped fresh coriander (cilantro)
1 tsp garam masala
salt and pepper

1 Melt the ghee over a medium heat in a large pan. Add the mustard seeds, and when they start to splutter, add the onion, garlic, carrot, and ginger. Cook until soft, about 5 minutes. Add the chilli and stir in the tomato purée (paste). Stir in the split peas.

2 Add the tomatoes and stock, and bring to the boil. Season well.

3 Simmer for 40 minutes, stirring occasionally. Add the pumpkin and cauliflower, and simmer for a further 30 minutes, covered, until the split peas are soft.

4 Meanwhile, heat the oil in a frying pan (skillet) over a high heat. Add the aubergine (eggplant), and stir until sealed on all sides. Remove and drain on paper towels.

5 Stir the aubergine (eggplant) into the split pea mixture with the coriander (cilantro) and garam masala. Check for seasoning.

6 Transfer to a serving dish and serve immediately.

Step *1*

Step *3*

Step *4*

Split Peas with Vegetables

Here is a simple, yet nourishing and flavourful way of cooking yellow split peas.
Vary the selection of vegetables and spices according to personal preferences.

SERVES 4–5

INGREDIENTS

250 g/8 oz/1 cup dried yellow split peas
1.25 litres/2 pints/5 cups cold water
½ tsp ground turmeric (optional)
500g/1 lb new potatoes, scrubbed
75 ml/5 tbsp/⅓ cup vegetable oil
2 onions, chopped coarsely
175 g/6 oz button mushrooms, wiped
1 tsp ground coriander
1 tsp ground cumin
1 tsp chilli powder
1 tsp garam masala
450 ml/¾ pint/1¾ cups vegetable stock
½ cauliflower, broken into florets
90 g/3 oz frozen peas
175 g/6 oz cherry tomatoes, halved
salt and pepper
mint sprigs, to garnish

1 Place the split peas in a bowl, add the cold water and leave to soak for at least 4 hours or overnight.

2 Place the peas and the soaking liquid in a fairly large saucepan, stir in the turmeric, if using, and bring to the boil. Skim off any surface scum, half-cover the pan with a lid and simmer gently for 20 minutes or until the peas are tender and almost dry. Remove from the heat and reserve.

3 Meanwhile, cut the potatoes into 5 mm (¼ inch) thick slices. Heat the oil in a flameproof casserole, add the onions, potatoes and mushrooms and cook gently for 5 minutes, stirring frequently. Stir in the spices and fry gently for 1 minute, then add salt and pepper to taste, stock and cauliflower florets.

4 Cover and simmer gently for 25 minutes or until the potato is tender, stirring occasionally. Add the split peas (and any of the cooking liquid) and the frozen peas. Bring to the boil, cover and cook for 5 minutes.

5 Stir in the cherry tomatoes and cook for 2 minutes. Taste and adjust the seasoning, if necessary. Serve hot, garnished with mint sprigs.

Step *2*

Step *3*

Step *5*

Channa Dal

This is a dish to consider next time you prepare a dal. Many types of dal (dried pulses and lentils) are used in India – yellow split peas is just one.

SERVES 4–6

INGREDIENTS

2 tbsp ghee
1 large onion, chopped finely
1 garlic clove, crushed
1 tbsp grated ginger root
1 tbsp cumin seeds, ground
2 tsp coriander seeds, ground
1 dried red chilli
2.5 cm/1 inch piece cinnamon stick
1 tsp salt
½ tsp ground turmeric
250 g/½ lb/1 cup yellow split peas,
soaked in cold water for 1 hour and drained
425 g /14 oz can plum tomatoes
300 ml/½ pint/1¼ cups water
2 tsp garam masala

1 Heat the ghee in a large saucepan, add the onion, garlic and ginger and fry for 3–4 minutes until the onion has softened slightly.

2 Add the cumin, coriander, chilli, cinnamon, salt and turmeric, then stir in the split peas and mix well.

3 Add the tomatoes, breaking them up slightly with the back of the spoon.

4 Add the water and bring to the boil. Reduce the heat to very low and simmer, uncovered, for about 40 minutes, stirring occasionally, until most of the liquid has been absorbed and the split peas are tender. Skim the surface occasionally with a perforated spoon to remove any scum.

5 Gradually stir in the garam masala, tasting after each addition, until it is of the required flavour.

Step *2*

Step *3*

Step *4*

Chick-Peas (Garbanzo Beans) & Aubergine (Eggplant) in Tomato Cream

Canned chick-peas (garbanzo beans) are used in this dish, but you could use black-eye beans or red kidney beans instead.

SERVES 4

INGREDIENTS

1 large aubergine (eggplant)
2 courgettes (zucchini)
6 tbsp vegetable ghee or oil
1 large onion, quartered and sliced
2 garlic cloves, crushed
1–2 fresh green chillies,
seeded and chopped,
or use 1–2 tsp minced chilli (from a jar)
2 tsp ground coriander
2 tsp cumin seeds
1 tsp ground turmeric
1 tsp garam masala
425 g/14 oz can chopped tomatoes
300 ml/½ pint/1¼ cups vegetable stock or water
salt and pepper
425 g/14 oz can chick-peas (garbanzo beans),
drained and rinsed
2 tbsp chopped fresh mint
150 ml/¼ pint/⅔ cup double (heavy) cream

1 Trim the leaf end off aubergine (eggplant) and cut into cubes. Trim and slice the courgettes (zucchini). Heat the ghee or oil in a saucepan and gently fry the aubergine (eggplant), courgettes (zucchini), onion, garlic and chillies for about 5 minutes, stirring frequently and adding a little more oil to the pan, if necessary.

2 Stir in the spices and cook for 30 seconds. Add the tomatoes, stock, and salt and pepper to taste. Cook for 10 minutes.

3 Add the chick-peas (garbanzo beans) to the pan and continue cooking for a further 5 minutes.

4 Stir in the mint and cream and reheat gently. Taste and adjust the seasoning, if necessary. Serve hot with plain or pilau rice, or with parathas, if preferred.

Step *1*

Step *2*

Step *4*

Kabli Channa Sag

Pulses such as chick-peas (garbanzo beans) are widely used in India, and this satisfying, earthy dish is characteristically easy to make and quite delicious.

SERVES 6

INGREDIENTS

250 g/8 oz/generous cup chick-peas
(garbanzo beans), soaked overnight
and drained
5 cloves
2.5 cm/1 inch piece cinnamon stick
2 garlic cloves
3 tbsp sunflower oil
1 small onion, sliced
3 tbsp lemon juice
1 tsp coriander seeds
2 tomatoes, peeled,
seeded and chopped
500 g/1 lb spinach, tough stems removed
1 tbsp chopped fresh coriander (cilantro)

TO GARNISH

fresh coriander (cilantro) sprigs
lemon slices

1 Put the chick-peas (garbanzo beans) into a saucepan with enough water to cover. Add the cloves, cinnamon and 1 garlic clove that has been lightly crushed with the back of a knife to release the juices. Bring to the boil, reduce the heat and simmer for 40–50 minutes, or until the chick-peas (garbanzo beans) are tender. Skim off any foam that comes to the surface.

2 Meanwhile, heat 1 tablespoon of the oil in a saucepan. Crush the remaining garlic clove. Put this into the pan with the oil and the onion, and cook over a moderate heat until soft, about 5 minutes.

3 Remove the cloves, cinnamon and garlic from the pan of chick-peas (garbanzo beans). Drain the chick-peas (garbanzo beans). Using a food processor or a fork, blend 90 g/3 oz/½ cup of the chick-peas (garbanzo beans) with the onion and garlic, the lemon juice and 1 tablespoon of the oil until smooth. Stir this purée into the remaining chick-peas (garbanzo beans).

4 Heat the remaining oil in a large frying pan (skillet), add the coriander seeds and stir for 1 minute. Stir in the tomatoes, then add the spinach. Cover and cook for 1 minute over a moderate heat. The spinach should be wilted, but not soggy. Stir in the chopped coriander (cilantro) and remove from the heat.

5 Transfer the chick-peas (garbanzo beans) to a serving dish, and spoon over the spinach. Garnish with the coriander (cilantro) and lemon.

Step *1*

Step *3*

Step *4*

Egg & Lentil Curry

A nutritious meal that is easy and relatively quick to make. The curried lentil sauce would also be delicious served with cooked vegetables.

SERVES 4

INGREDIENTS

3 tbsp vegetable ghee or oil
1 large onion, chopped
2 garlic cloves, chopped
2.5 cm/1 inch ginger root, chopped finely
½ tsp minced chilli (from a jar),
or use chilli powder
1 tsp ground coriander
1 tsp ground cumin
1 tsp paprika
90 g/3 oz red lentils
450 ml /¾ pint/1¾ cups vegetable stock
250 g/8 oz can chopped tomatoes
6 eggs
50 ml/2 fl oz/¼ cup coconut milk
salt

TO GARNISH

2 tomatoes, cut into wedges
coriander (cilantro) sprigs

TO SERVE

parathas, chapatis or naan bread

1 Heat the ghee or oil in a saucepan, add the onion and fry gently for 3 minutes. Stir in the garlic, ginger, chilli and spices and cook gently for 1 minute, stirring frequently. Stir in the lentils, stock and chopped tomatoes and bring to the boil. Reduce the heat, cover and simmer gently for 30 minutes, stirring occasionally until the lentils and onion are tender.

2 Meanwhile, put the eggs in a saucepan of cold water and bring to the boil. Reduce the heat and simmer for 10 minutes. Drain and cover immediately with cold water.

3 Stir the coconut milk into the lentil mixture and season well with salt to taste. Purée the mixture in a blender or food processor until smooth or push through a coarse sieve. Return to the pan and heat through.

4 Shell and cut the hard-boiled eggs in half lengthways. Arrange 3 halves, in a petal design, on each serving plate. Spoon the hot lentil sauce over the eggs, adding enough to flood the serving plate. Arrange a tomato wedge and a coriander (cilantro) sprig between each halved egg. Serve hot with parathas, chapatis or naan bread to mop up the sauce.

Step *1*

Step *3*

Step *4*

Tarka Dal

*This is just one version of many dals that are served throughout India;
in the absence of regular supplies of meat, they form a staple part of the diet.*

SERVES 4

INGREDIENTS

2 tbsp ghee
2 shallots, sliced
1 tsp yellow mustard seeds
2 garlic cloves, crushed
8 fenugreek seeds
1 cm/½ inch piece ginger root, grated
½ tsp salt
125 g/4 oz/½ cup red lentils
1 tbsp tomato purée (paste)
600 ml/1 pint/2½ cups water
2 tomatoes, peeled and chopped
1 tbsp lemon juice
4 tbsp chopped fresh coriander (cilantro)
½ tsp chilli powder
½ tsp garam masala
naan bread, to serve

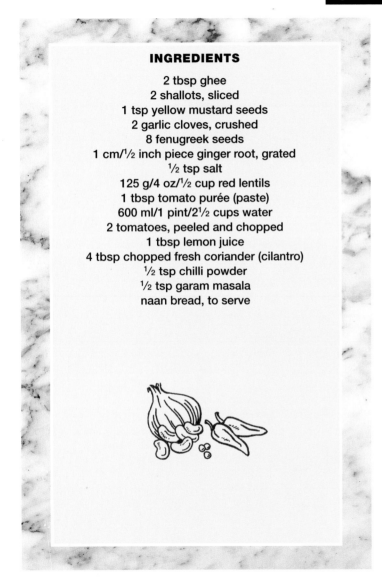

1 Heat half the ghee in a large saucepan, and add the shallots. Cook for 2–3 minutes over a high heat, then add the mustard seeds. Cover the pan until the seeds begin to pop.

2 Immediately remove the lid from the pan and add the garlic, fenugreek, ginger and salt.

3 Stir once and add the lentils, tomato purée (paste) and water and simmer gently for 10 minutes.

4 Stir in the tomatoes, lemon juice, and coriander (cilantro) and simmer for a further 4–5 minutes until the lentils are tender.

5 Transfer to a serving dish. Heat the remaining ghee in a small saucepan until it starts to bubble. Remove from the heat and stir in the garam masala and chilli powder. Immediately pour over the tarka dal and serve.

Step *1*

Step *2*

Step *3*

Dal with Spinach

Green lentils are cooked in a delicious blend of spinach, onion, garlic and spices. Okra is known as bhindi or ladies' fingers.

SERVES 4

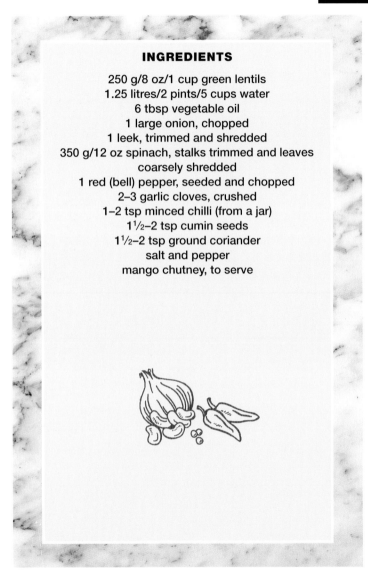

INGREDIENTS

250 g/8 oz/1 cup green lentils
1.25 litres/2 pints/5 cups water
6 tbsp vegetable oil
1 large onion, chopped
1 leek, trimmed and shredded
350 g/12 oz spinach, stalks trimmed and leaves
coarsely shredded
1 red (bell) pepper, seeded and chopped
2–3 garlic cloves, crushed
1–2 tsp minced chilli (from a jar)
1½–2 tsp cumin seeds
1½–2 tsp ground coriander
salt and pepper
mango chutney, to serve

1 Place the lentils in a sieve and rinse well under cold running water. Drain, then place in a saucepan with the water. Cover and cook for 30 minutes until the lentils are tender and the liquid has been absorbed.

2 Meanwhile, heat the oil in a large saucepan and add the onion, leek, spinach and red (bell) pepper. Fry gently for 8 minutes, stirring and turning frequently until the spinach has wilted.

3 Stir in the garlic, chilli and spices and fry gently for a further 2 minutes.

4 When the lentils are cooked, uncover and shake the pan over a moderate heat for a few moments to dry off. Add the lentils to the spinach and onion mixture and toss together. Season with salt and pepper to taste and serve hot, with mango chutney.

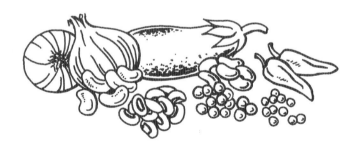

Step *2*

Step *3*

Step *4*

Murkha Dal

With this dal recipe, the garlic is intended to burn in the bottom of the pan, so that the flavour permeates the dish.

SERVES 4

INGREDIENTS

60 g/2 oz/¼ cup butter
2 tsp black mustard seeds
1 onion, chopped finely
2 garlic cloves, chopped finely
1 tbsp grated ginger root
1 tsp turmeric
2 green chillies,
seeded and chopped finely
250 g/8 oz/1 cup red lentils
1 litre/1¾ pints/4 cups water
300 ml/½ pint/1¼ cups coconut milk
1 tsp salt

1 Melt the butter in a large saucepan over a moderate heat. Add the mustard seeds and cover the pan. When you can hear the seeds popping, add the onion, garlic and ginger. Cook, uncovered, until they are soft and the garlic is brown, about 7–8 minutes.

2 Stir in the turmeric and chillies and cook for 1–2 minutes until the chillies soften a little.

3 Add the lentils and cook for 2 minutes, stirring frequently, until the lentils begin to turn translucent.

4 Add the water, coconut milk and salt. Stir well. Bring to the boil, then reduce the heat and simmer for 40 minutes or until the desired consistency is reached. Cook the dal for longer if you prefer a thicker consistency. However, if you intend to reheat it later rather than eat it straight away, cook for only 30 minutes to allow for reheating time.

5 Serve immediately, while piping hot.

Step *1*

Step *3*

Step *4*

BREADS

Bread is another staple ingredient in India, used to mop up sauces and stews, and to make meals easier to eat with the hands. It is usually eaten hot, or within a few minutes of cooking.

With one or two exceptions, Indian breads are unleavened, that is they do not contain any raising agent. The flours are usually unrefined and often milled from grains other than wheat, including millet, barley and white maize. Many people grind their flours at home by hand.

Since it is unleavened, Indian bread is very easy to make as it needs very little kneading and rising. Most breads are flat, usually circular in shape, often resembling griddle scones or pancakes. Some are dry-fried or fried with a little oil, others are deep-fried into wonderfully puffy hollow shells.

Breads appear in many forms – pooris, poppadoms, oven-baked naan, pan-fried chapatis and parathas – all equally delicious.

Peshwari Naan

***A tandoor oven throws out a ferocious heat; for an authentic effect, leave
your grill (broiler) on for a long time before the first dough goes on.***

SERVES 4–6

INGREDIENTS

50 ml/2 fl oz/½ cup warm water
pinch of sugar
½ tsp active dried yeast
500 g/1 lb/4 cups strong white flour
½ tsp salt
50 ml/2 fl oz/¼ cup natural yogurt
2 crisp, green apples, peeled, cooked and puréed
60 g/2 oz/⅓ cup sultanas (golden raisins)
60 g/2 oz/½ cup flaked (slivered) almonds
1 tbsp coriander (cilantro) leaves
2 tbsp grated coconut

1 Combine the water and sugar in a bowl and sprinkle over the yeast. Leave for 5–10 minutes, until the yeast has dissolved and the mixture is foamy.

2 Put the flour and salt into a large bowl and make a well in the centre. Add the yeast mixture and yogurt to the bowl. Draw the flour into the liquid, until all the flour is absorbed. Mix together, adding enough tepid water to form a soft dough, about 150 ml/¼ pint/⅔ cup.

3 Turn out on to a floured board and knead for 10 minutes until smooth and elastic. Put into an oiled bowl, cover with a cloth and leave for 3 hours in a warm place, or in the fridge overnight. Line the grill (broiler) pan with foil, shiny side up.

4 Divide the dough into 4 pieces and roll each piece out to a 20 cm/8 inch oval.

5 Pull one end out into a teardrop shape, about 5 mm/¼ inch thick. Lay on a floured surface and prick all over with a fork.

6 Brush both sides of the bread with oil. Place under a preheated grill (broiler) at the highest setting. Cook for 3 minutes, turn the bread over and cook for a further 3 minutes. It should have dark brown spots all over.

7 Spread a teaspoonful of the apple purée all over the bread, then sprinkle over a quarter of the sultanas (golden raisins), the flaked (slivered) almonds, the coriander (cilantro) leaves and the coconut. Repeat with the remaining 3 ovals of dough.

Step *4*

Step *5*

Step *7*

Spicy Oven Bread

This Western-style bread has been adapted with Indian ingredients.
It is quite a rich mix and very tasty.

SERVES 4

INGREDIENTS

½ tsp active dried yeast
300 ml/½ pint/1¼ cups warm water
500 g/1 lb/4 cups strong white flour
1 tsp salt
250 g/8 oz/1 cup butter, melted and cooled
½ tsp garam masala
½ tsp coriander seeds, ground
1 tsp cumin seeds, ground

1 Mix the yeast with a little of the warm water until it starts to foam and is completely dissolved.

2 Put the flour and salt into a large bowl, make a well in the centre and add the yeast mixture, and 125 g/ 4 oz/½ cup of the melted butter. Blend the yeast and butter together before drawing in the flour and kneading lightly. Gradually add enough water to form a firm dough – you may not need it all.

3 Turn the dough out and knead until smooth and elastic, about 10 minutes. Put the dough into an oiled bowl, turning to coat. Cover and leave in a warm place to rise until doubled, about 30 minutes. Alternatively, leave in the refrigerator overnight.

4 Knock back (punch down) the dough and divide into 8 balls. Roll each ball out to about a 15 cm/6 inch round. Put on to a floured baking sheet. Sprinkle with flour and leave for 20 minutes.

5 Mix the spices with the remaining melted butter.

6 Brush each bread with the spice and butter mixture and cover with foil. Place on the middle shelf of a preheated oven at 220°C/425°F/Gas mark 7 for 5 minutes. Remove the foil, brush with the butter once again and cook for a further 5 minutes.

7 Remove from the oven and wrap in a clean tea towel (dish cloth) until ready to eat.

Step *2*

Step *4*

Step *6*

Parathas

These triangular-shaped breads are so easy to make and are the perfect addition
to most Indian meals. Serve hot, spread with a little butter, if wished.

MAKES 6

INGREDIENTS

90 g/3 oz/³/₄ cup plain wholemeal
(whole wheat) flour
90 g/3 oz/³/₄ cup plain white flour
a good pinch of salt
1 tbsp vegetable oil, plus extra for greasing
75 ml/3 fl oz/¹/₃ cup tepid water

1 Place the flours and the salt in a bowl. Drizzle 1 tablespoon of oil over the flour, add the tepid water and mix to form a soft dough, adding a little more water, if necessary. Knead on a lightly floured surface until smooth, then cover and leave for 30 minutes.

2 Knead the dough on a floured surface and divide into 6 equal pieces. Shape each one into a ball. Roll out on a floured surface to a 15 cm/6 inch round and brush very lightly with oil.

3 Fold in half, and then in half again to form a triangle. Roll out to form an 18 cm/7 inch triangle (when measured from point to centre top), dusting with extra flour as necessary.

4 Brush a large frying pan with a little oil and heat until hot, then add one or two parathas and cook for about 1–1¹/₂ minutes. Brush the surfaces very lightly with oil, then turn and cook the other sides for 1¹/₂ minutes until cooked through.

5 Place the cooked parathas on a plate and cover with foil, or place between a clean tea towel to keep warm, while cooking the remainder in the same way, greasing the pan between cooking each batch.

Step *2*

Step *3*

Step *4*

Stuffed Parathas

To make parathas successfully, be sure to knead the dough until it is quite
smooth and to roll it out as thinly as you can.

SERVES 4–8

INGREDIENTS

250 g/8 oz/2 cups plain wholemeal
(whole wheat) flour
250 g/8 oz/2 cups plain (all purpose) flour
120–180 ml/4–6 fl oz/½–¾ cup water
1 tbsp ghee
1 onion, chopped
2.5 cm/1 inch piece cinnamon stick
1 bay leaf
1 dried red chilli
¼ tsp ground turmeric
1 tsp coriander seeds, ground
1 tsp cumin seeds, ground
500 g/1 lb/2 cups lean minced (ground) beef
150 ml/¼ pint/⅔ cup natural yogurt
125 g/4 oz/¾ cup frozen peas
60 g/2 oz/¼ cup butter, melted
salt and pepper
chopped fresh coriander (cilantro), to garnish

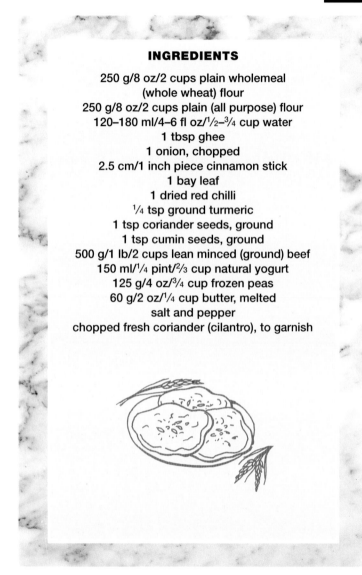

1 Sift the two flours and a pinch of salt together into a bowl and make a well in the centre.

2 Gradually add water to make a soft dough, and knead until smooth and no longer sticky. Set aside.

3 Heat the ghee in a large frying pan (skillet) and fry the onion until golden brown. Add the cinnamon, bay leaf, chilli, turmeric, coriander, cumin and minced (ground) beef, and stir for 1 minute. Add the yogurt and cook over a high heat until the beef is dry. Add the peas, season to taste, then simmer for 8–10 minutes.

4 To make the parathas, divide the dough into 6 or 8 pieces. Roll each piece into a ball, then roll out to a 25 cm/10 inch round.

5 Brush the upper side with melted butter. Fold in half, and spoon 1 tablespoon of the stuffing into the centre of each folded piece. Fold each half in half again so that you are left with cone shapes.

6 Gently heat a large frying pan (skillet) and place a paratha in it. Brush each side lightly with a little melted butter and cook over a medium heat for 3–4 minutes. Do not let the pan get too hot. Turn over and cook the other side for 3–4 minutes. Keep warm and repeat with the remaining parathas. Serve immediately.

Step *1*

Step *4*

Step *5*

Prawn (Shrimp) Pooris

Tiger prawns (shrimp) are especially good cooked this way, although the less expensive, smaller peeled prawns (shrimp) may be used instead.

SERVES 6

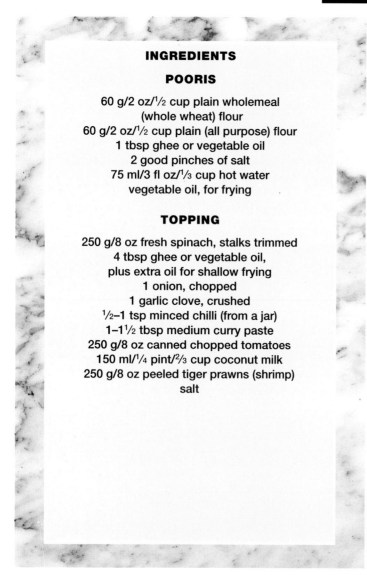

INGREDIENTS

POORIS

60 g/2 oz/½ cup plain wholemeal
(whole wheat) flour
60 g/2 oz/½ cup plain (all purpose) flour
1 tbsp ghee or vegetable oil
2 good pinches of salt
75 ml/3 fl oz/⅓ cup hot water
vegetable oil, for frying

TOPPING

250 g/8 oz fresh spinach, stalks trimmed
4 tbsp ghee or vegetable oil,
plus extra oil for shallow frying
1 onion, chopped
1 garlic clove, crushed
½–1 tsp minced chilli (from a jar)
1–1½ tbsp medium curry paste
250 g/8 oz canned chopped tomatoes
150 ml/¼ pint/⅔ cup coconut milk
250 g/8 oz peeled tiger prawns (shrimp)
salt

1 To make the pooris, put the flours in a bowl and make a well in the centre. Add the ghee or oil, salt and hot water and mix to form a dough. Leave to stand for 1 hour.

2 Meanwhile, prepare the topping. Cut the spinach crossways into wide strips – do this by making bundles of leaves and slicing with a sharp knife.

3 Heat the ghee or oil in a frying pan, add the onion, garlic, chilli and spinach and cook gently for 4 minutes, shaking the pan and stirring frequently. Add the curry paste, tomatoes and coconut milk and simmer for 10 minutes, stirring occasionally. Remove from the heat, stir in the prawns (shrimp) and season with salt.

4 Knead the dough well on a floured surface, divide into 6 pieces and shape into 6 balls. Roll out each one to a 12 cm/5 inch round. Heat about 2.5 cm/1 inch oil in a deep frying pan until smoking hot. Take one poori at a time, lower into the hot oil and cook for 10–15 seconds on each side until puffed up and golden. Remove the poori with a slotted spoon, drain on absorbent paper towels and keep warm while cooking the remainder in the same way.

5 Reheat the prawn (shrimp) mixture, stirring until piping hot. Arrange a poori on each serving plate and spoon the prawn (shrimp) and spinach mixture on to each one. Serve immediately.

Step *1*

Step *4*

Step *5*

Mixed (Bell) Pepper Pooris

*Wholemeal (wholewheat) pooris are easy to make and so good to eat
served with a topping of spicy mixed (bell) peppers and yogurt.*

SERVES 6

INGREDIENTS

POORIS

125 g/4 oz/ 1 cup plain wholemeal
(whole wheat) flour
1 tbsp vegetable ghee or oil
2 good pinches of salt
75 ml/3 fl oz/⅓ cup hot water
vegetable oil, for shallow frying
natural yogurt, to serve
coriander (cilantro) sprigs, to garnish

TOPPING

4 tbsp vegetable ghee or oil
1 large onion, quartered and thinly sliced
½ red (bell) pepper,
seeded and thinly sliced
½ green (bell) pepper,
seeded and thinly sliced
¼ aubergine (eggplant),
cut lengthways into 6 wedges and sliced thinly
1 garlic clove, crushed
2.5 cm/1 in ginger root, chopped finely
½–1 tsp minced chilli (from a jar)
2 tsp mild or medium curry paste
250 g/8 oz can chopped tomatoes
salt

1 To make the pooris, put the flour in a bowl with the ghee or oil and salt. Add hot water and mix to form a fairly soft dough. Knead gently, cover with a damp cloth and leave for 30 minutes.

2 Meanwhile, prepare the topping. Heat the ghee or oil in a large saucepan, add the onion, (bell) peppers, aubergine (eggplant), garlic, ginger, chilli and curry paste and fry gently for 5 minutes. Stir in the tomatoes and salt to taste. Simmer gently, uncovered, for 5 minutes, stirring occasionally until the sauce thickens. Remove from the heat.

3 Knead the dough on a floured surface. Divide into 6. Roll each piece to a round about 15 cm/6 in in diameter. Cover each one as you finish rolling, to prevent drying out.

4 Heat about 1 cm/½ in oil in a large frying pan. Add the pooris, one at a time, and fry for about 15 seconds on each side until puffed and golden, turning frequently. Drain on paper towels and keep warm while cooking the remainder in the same way.

5 Reheat the vegetable mixture. Place a poori on each serving plate and top with the vegetable mixture. Add a spoonful of yogurt to each one and garnish with coriander (cilantro) sprigs. Serve hot.

Step *1*

Step *3*

Step *5*

Spinach Poori

These little nibbles are very satisfying to make. Don't be slow in serving them and they will still be little puffballs when you get to the table.

SERVES 6

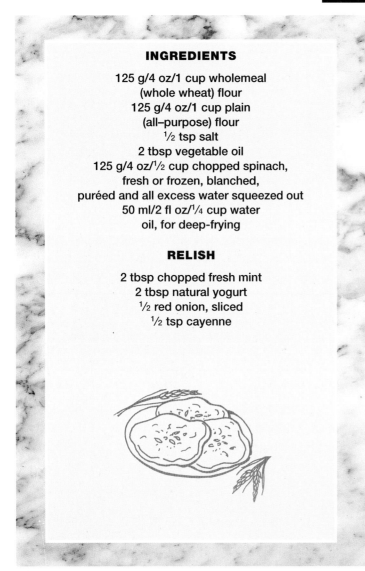

INGREDIENTS

125 g/4 oz/1 cup wholemeal
(whole wheat) flour
125 g/4 oz/1 cup plain
(all–purpose) flour
½ tsp salt
2 tbsp vegetable oil
125 g/4 oz/½ cup chopped spinach,
fresh or frozen, blanched,
puréed and all excess water squeezed out
50 ml/2 fl oz/¼ cup water
oil, for deep-frying

RELISH

2 tbsp chopped fresh mint
2 tbsp natural yogurt
½ red onion, sliced
½ tsp cayenne

1 Sift the flours and salt together into a bowl. Drizzle over the oil and rub in until the mixture resembles fine breadcrumbs.

2 Add the spinach and enough water to make a stiff dough. Knead for 10 minutes until smooth.

3 Form the dough into a ball. Put into an oiled bowl and turn to coat. Cover with clingfilm (plastic wrap) and set aside for 30 minutes.

4 Meanwhile make the relish. Combine the mint, yogurt and onion, transfer to a serving bowl and sift the cayenne over the top.

5 Knead the dough again and divide into 12 small balls. Remove 1 ball and keep the rest covered. Roll this ball out into a 12 cm/5 inch circle.

6 Put the oil into a wok or wide frying pan (skillet) to 2.5 cm/1 inch depth. Heat it until a haze appears. It must be very hot.

7 Have ready a plate lined with paper towels. Put 1 poori on the surface of the oil – if it sinks, it should rise up immediately and sizzle; if it doesn't, the oil isn't hot enough. Keep the poori submerged in the oil, using the back of a fish slice or a perforated spoon. The poori will puff up immediately. Turn it over and cook the other side for 5–10 seconds.

8 As soon as the poori is cooked, remove and drain. Repeat with the remaining balls of dough.

Step *2*

Step *5*

Step *7*

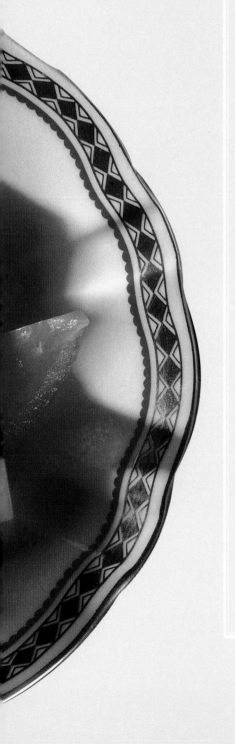

CHUTNEYS, PICKLES & RELISHES

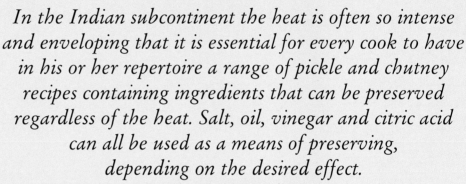

In the Indian subcontinent the heat is often so intense and enveloping that it is essential for every cook to have in his or her repertoire a range of pickle and chutney recipes containing ingredients that can be preserved regardless of the heat. Salt, oil, vinegar and citric acid can all be used as a means of preserving, depending on the desired effect.

These preserves have claimed their place in the grand scheme of Indian gastronomy – no table would be complete without a selection of pickles presented on a tray for you to dip into. Who can imagine eating a dry, spicy, tender dish without a yogurt accompaniment? Or crisp poppadoms without the mango chutney? Not only do Indian pickles and preserves accompany meat and fish, but because vegetarianism is such a way of life in India, they are devised to complement the meat-free meals too.

Chilli Chutney

Surprisingly enough an Indian meal isn't always hot enough for everybody. This chutney will give a bite to the meal, as well as a zingy lime freshener to the palate.

SERVES 6

INGREDIENTS

1 lime, halved and
sliced very thinly
1 tbsp salt
2 red chillies, chopped finely
2 green chillies, chopped finely
1 tbsp white wine vinegar
1 tbsp lemon juice
½ tsp sugar
2 shallots, chopped finely
1 tbsp oil

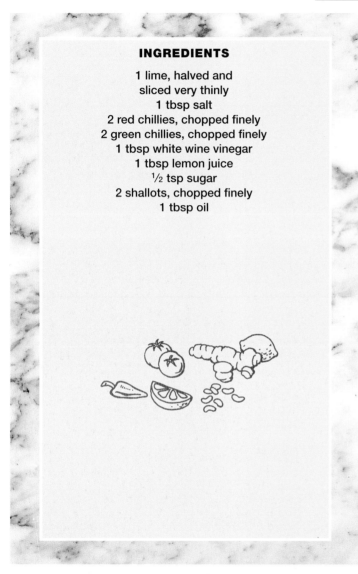

1 Combine the lime slices with the salt. Leave to stand for 30 minutes.

2 Mix the chillies with the vinegar. Stir for a few seconds, then drain.

3 Mix together the chillies, lemon juice, sugar, chopped shallots and oil.

4 Add the salted limes to the chilli mixture, mixing thoroughly.

5 Transfer the chutney to a non-staining serving dish. Serve as an accompaniment to any mild or rich curry.

Step *1*

Step *3*

Step *4*

Walnut Chutney

This delicious chutney complements the Butterfly Prawns (Shrimp) on
page 20. The Garlic Chutney has a hotter flavour.

SERVES 4–6

INGREDIENTS

60 g/2 oz/½ cup shelled walnuts
200 ml/7 fl oz/scant 1 cup natural yogurt
2 tbsp chopped fresh coriander (cilantro)
1 green chilli, chopped
1 garlic clove, chopped finely
salt
fresh coriander (cilantro), sprig to garnish

GARLIC CHUTNEY

10 garlic cloves
100 g/4 oz/1 cup raw peanuts
2 tbsp desiccated (shredded) coconut
3 green chillies, chopped
4 tbsp lemon juice
1 tsp ground cumin
1 tsp ground coriander
salt

1 Grind in a spice grinder or chop finely by hand 30 g/1 oz/¼ cup of the walnuts. Chop the remaining walnuts roughly by hand.

2 Combine the chopped and ground walnuts, mixing thoroughly.

3 Stir in the yogurt, coriander (cilantro), chilli and garlic. Season to taste. You will find the chutney thickens a lot at this stage. Transfer to a serving dish and garnish with coriander (cilantro). This will keep for 1–2 days in the refrigerator.

4 To make the Garlic Chutney, put all the ingredients into a pestle and mortar, or food processor, and grind with enough water to make a paste.

5 Leave to stand for an hour before serving. This will keep for 1–2 days in the refrigerator.

Step *1*

Step *2*

Step *3*

Lime Pickle

This is the hottest and most thirst-making of the Indian pickles. Ginger pickle is the sweetest, but lime pickle is the one that will have you going back for more.

SERVES 8

INGREDIENTS

6 limes, quartered
60 g/2 oz/½ cup salt
1 tbsp yellow mustard seeds
1 tsp fenugreek seeds
seeds from 2 star anise
4 small green chillies, chopped finely
125 g/4 oz/¾ cup light muscovado sugar
1 tbsp ground ginger
3–4 tbsp water

1 Put the limes into a large bowl and sprinkle over the salt. Leave for 24 hours.

2 Next day, put the mustard seeds, fenugreek, star anise seeds and chillies into a saucepan and cover. Place over a high heat and roast the spices, shaking the pan constantly until the mustard seeds start to pop. Remove from the heat.

3 Strain the liquid from the limes into a small pan. Add the sugar, ginger and water. Boil for 2 minutes or until the sugar has dissolved.

4 Combine the limes and spices and put into 2 clean, dry preserving jars. Pour over the sugar solution, making sure that it covers the limes. If it doesn't, cram the limes further down into the jar, or remove one or two quarters.

5 Cover the jars loosely, and when quite cool, screw on the lids tightly. Label each jar, adding the date on which the pickle was made. Keep in a cool place for 4 weeks before using.

Step *2*

Step *3*

Step *4*

Tomato, Onion & Cucumber Kachumber

This is a relish that is served at all Indian tables as a palate refresher or an appetizer. Two variations on the main recipe are included here.

SERVES 6

INGREDIENTS

3 ripe tomatoes, peeled
¼ cucumber, peeled
1 small onion, quartered
1 tsp lime juice
2 green chillies, seeded and chopped
(optional)

MANGO KACHUMBER

½ mango, peeled and chopped
1 small onion, chopped
1 tbsp chopped fresh coriander (cilantro)
2 tomatoes, chopped

RADISH KACHUMBER

8 large radishes, sliced
½ cucumber, peeled and chopped
1 small onion, chopped
1 tbsp chopped fresh coriander (cilantro)
1 tbsp oil
1 tbsp vinegar

1 Cut the tomatoes into quarters, then cut each quarter in half lengthways. The seeds can be removed at this stage, if you prefer.

2 Cut the cucumber lengthways into quarters. Remove the seeds, and cut the flesh into cubes.

3 Cut each onion quarter into slices.

4 Combine all the ingredients in a bowl and sprinkle with lime juice. Add the chillies, if using, and serve.

MANGO KACHUMBER

1 Combine all the ingredients in a bowl, and serve.

RADISH KACHUMBER

1 Combine all the ingredients in a bowl, and serve.

Step *1*

Step *2*

Step *3*

Cucumber Raita

In any Indian restaurant, the first thing to be brought to the table should be a kachumber salad and a raita, which you eat with a few poppadoms.

SERVES 4

INGREDIENTS

2 tsp fresh mint
½ cucumber
250 ml/8 fl oz/1 cup natural yogurt
salt and pepper
freshly grated nutmeg, to garnish

GRAPEFRUIT RAITA

1 tsp sugar
1 tsp finely grated grapefruit rind
½ grapefruit, segmented
250 ml/8 fl oz/1 cup natural yogurt
salt and pepper

MELON RAITA

¼ honeydew or firm melon, peeled and cut into
1 cm/½ inch cubes
¼ medium pineapple, peeled and cut into
1 cm/½ inch cubes
1 tsp cayenne
1 tsp ground coriander seeds
250 ml/8 fl oz/1 cup natural yogurt
salt and pepper

DATE RAITA

6 dates, chopped
1 tbsp raisins
1 crisp green apple, chopped
250 ml/8 fl oz/1 cup natural yogurt
salt and pepper

1 Chop the mint finely using a sharp knife.

2 Peel the cucumber, remove the seeds and cut the flesh into matchsticks.

3 Combine the cucumber with the yogurt and mint. Season with salt and pepper to taste.

4 Turn the mixture into a serving dish and sprinkle with nutmeg before serving.

GRAPEFRUIT RAITA

1 Combine all the ingredients and serve immediately. This version should be eaten on the day you make it, as it does not keep well.

MELON RAITA

1 Combine the melon and pineapple cubes, cayenne, ground coriander seeds, and salt and pepper in a bowl. Stir in the yogurt and serve. This will keep for 1–2 days in the refrigerator.

DATE RAITA

1 Combine all these ingredients in a bowl and serve. This will keep for 1–2 days in the refrigerator.

Step *1*

Step *2*

Step *3*

DESSERTS

Indian-style meals are traditionally rounded off with
something very sweet or with a large selection of
carefully prepared plain fresh fruit, such as mangoes,
guavas, melon and pears. These are best served well
chilled, especially in the summer months and can make
a welcome change or contrast to a spicy, warm, aromatic
main course feast.

For a stunning finale to an Indian meal, dice, slice or cut
the fruit into colourful wedges then arrange them on a
huge platter with sprigs of mint.

The simplest, and often most appreciated dessert is a
cooling kulfi or ice-cream. Many are served plain but
others are flavoured with mango and coconut. They are
delicious sprinkled with chopped shelled
pistachios or almonds.

Mango Ice-Cream

*This delicious ice-cream with its refreshing tang of mango and lime
makes the perfect ending to a hot and spicy meal.*

SERVES 4–6

INGREDIENTS

150 ml/¼ pint/⅔ cup single cream
2 egg yolks
½ tsp cornflour (cornstarch)
1 tsp water
2 × 425 g/14 oz cans mango slices in syrup,
drained
1 tbsp lime or lemon juice
150 ml/¼ pint/⅔ cup double (heavy) cream
mint sprigs, to decorate

1 Heat the single cream in a saucepan until hot (but do not allow it to boil). Place the egg yolks in a bowl with the cornflour (cornstarch) and water and mix together until smooth. Pour the hot cream on to the egg yolk mixture, stirring all the time.

2 Return the mixture to the pan and place over a very low heat, whisking or stirring all the time until the mixture thickens and coats the back of a wooden spoon. (Do not try and hurry this process or the mixture will overcook and spoil.) Pour into a bowl.

3 Purée the drained mango slices in a blender or food processor until smooth, or chop finely, mash with a fork and push through a sieve. Mix with the custard and stir in the lime juice. Whip the double (heavy) cream until soft peaks form. Fold into the mango mixture until thoroughly combined.

4 Transfer the mixture to a loaf tin or shallow freezerproof container. Cover and freeze for 2–3 hours or until half-frozen and still mushy in the centre. Turn the mixture into a bowl and mash well with a fork until smooth. Return to the container, cover and freeze again until firm.

5 Transfer the container of ice-cream to the main compartment of the refrigerator for about 30 minutes before serving to allow it to soften slightly. Scoop or spoon the ice-cream into serving dishes and decorate with mint sprigs.

Step *1*

Step *2*

Step *4*

Bananas with Spiced Yogurt & Almonds

*This simple but delicious dessert is at its nicest when made with
thick and creamy yogurt.*

SERVES 4-6

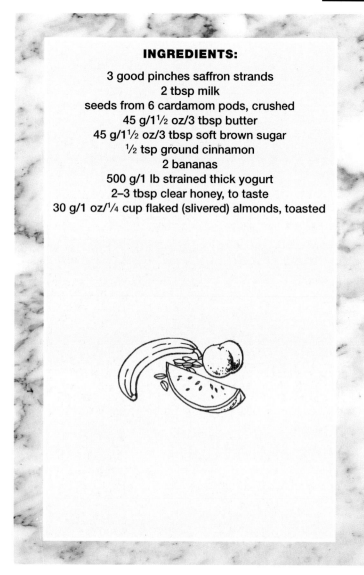

INGREDIENTS:

3 good pinches saffron strands
2 tbsp milk
seeds from 6 cardamom pods, crushed
45 g/1½ oz/3 tbsp butter
45 g/1½ oz/3 tbsp soft brown sugar
½ tsp ground cinnamon
2 bananas
500 g/1 lb strained thick yogurt
2–3 tbsp clear honey, to taste
30 g/1 oz/¼ cup flaked (slivered) almonds, toasted

1 Place the saffron strands on a small piece of foil and toast very lightly. Crush the saffron strands finely and place in a small bowl.

2 Add the milk and crushed cardamom seeds, stir well and leave to cool.

3 Meanwhile, melt the butter in a frying pan, add the sugar and cinnamon and stir well. Peel and slice the bananas and fry gently for about 1 minute, turning halfway through cooking. Remove from the pan and place the fried banana slices in decorative serving glasses.

4 Mix the yogurt with the cold spiced milk and the honey. Spoon the mixture on top of the bananas and liberally sprinkle the surface of each serving with toasted flaked (slivered) almonds. Chill before serving, if wished.

Step *1*

Step *2*

Step *4*

Coconut Ice-Cream

This delicious ice-cream will make the perfect ending to any Indian meal.
For a smooth-textured dessert leave out the coconut.

SERVES 6

INGREDIENTS

150 g/5 oz/²⁄₃ cup granulated sugar
300 ml/¹⁄₄ pint/1¹⁄₄ cups water
2 × 400 ml/14 fl oz cans coconut milk
300 ml/¹⁄₂ pint/1¹⁄₄ cups double (heavy) cream
2 tbsp desiccated (shredded) coconut
sprigs of mint or rose petals, to decorate

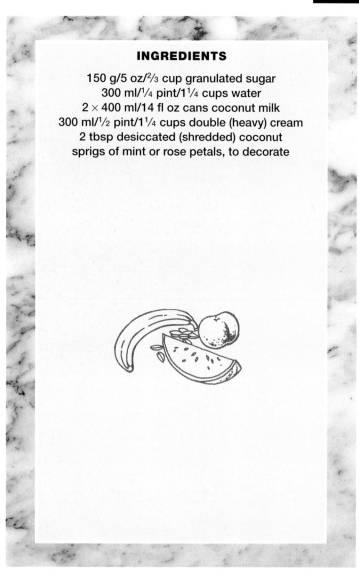

1 Place the sugar and water in a saucepan and heat gently, stirring occasionally until the sugar dissolves. Boil gently for 10 minutes without stirring, then remove from the heat and allow to cool slightly.

2 Mix the cooled syrup with the coconut milk and pour into a shallow freezer container. Cover and freeze for about 3 hours or until semi-frozen around the edges and mushy in the centre.

3 Transfer the mixture to a bowl and cut up with a knife, then place (half the quantity at a time) in a food processor and process until smooth, or whisk thoroughly by hand.

4 Turn the mixture into a bowl. Whip the cream until soft peaks form and fold into the ice-cream, then stir in the desiccated coconut. Return the mixture to the container and freeze again until solid.

5 Before serving, put the container in the refrigerator and leave in for 30 minutes (or at room temperature for 15 minutes) to soften. Scoop or spoon the ice-cream into serving dishes and decorate with sprigs of mint.

Step *2*

Step *3*

Step *4*

Mango & Yogurt Cream

This wonderfully refreshing dessert is designed to help refresh the palate after a hot and spicy meal.

SERVES 6

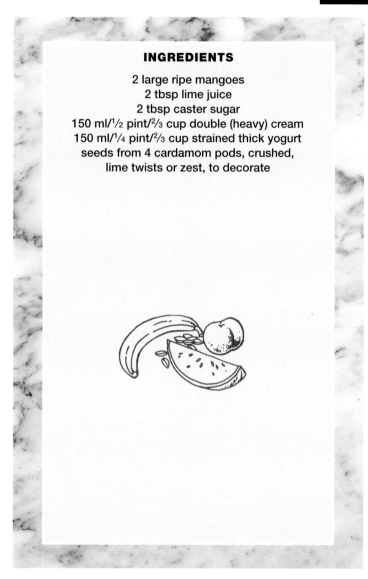

INGREDIENTS

2 large ripe mangoes
2 tbsp lime juice
2 tbsp caster sugar
150 ml/½ pint/⅔ cup double (heavy) cream
150 ml/¼ pint/⅔ cup strained thick yogurt
seeds from 4 cardamom pods, crushed,
lime twists or zest, to decorate

1 To prepare each mango, cut along either side of the large central stone, to give two halves of mango. Cut off any flesh attached to the stone, and remove the peel.

2 Place the flesh in a blender or food processor with the lime juice and sugar and process until the mixture forms a smooth purée, or chop the flesh, mash with a fork and push through a sieve. Turn the mixture into a bowl.

3 Whip the cream in a bowl until stiff, then fold in the yogurt and the crushed cardamom seeds.

4 Reserve 4 tablespoons of the mango purée for decoration, and mix the remaining mango purée into the cream and yogurt mixture.

5 Spoon the mixture into pretty serving glasses. Drizzle a little of the reserved mango sauce over each dessert and serve chilled, decorated with lime twists.

Step *1*

Step *3*

Step *4*

Indian Ice-Cream (Kulfi)

To make traditional Kulfi is quite a time-consuming process,
so why not try this deliciously easy version instead?

SERVES 6–8

INGREDIENTS

75 ml/3 fl oz/⅓ cup boiling water
4 cardamom pods,
crushed and seeds removed
425 g/14 oz can sweetened
condensed milk
75 ml/3 fl oz/⅓ cup cold water
30 g/1 oz/¼ cup unsalted pistachio nuts
30 g/1 oz/¼ cup blanched almonds
2 drops almond essence (optional)
150 ml/¼ pint/⅔ cup double (heavy) cream
lime zest and rose petals (optional),
to decorate

1 Pour the boiling water into a bowl, stir in the cardamom seeds and leave for 15 minutes to infuse.

2 Meanwhile, put the condensed milk into a blender or food processor together with the cold water, pistachio nuts, almonds and almond essence, if using. Process the mixture for about 30 seconds until very finely mixed.

3 Add the cooled and strained cardamom water and pour into a bowl. Whip the cream until soft peaks form. Whisk into the mixture. Pour into a shallow metal or plastic container and freeze for about 3 hours or until semi-frozen around the edges and mushy in the centre.

4 Transfer the mixture to a bowl and mash well with a fork (to break up the ice crystals). Divide the mixture evenly between 6–8 small moulds and freeze for at least 4 hours or overnight until firm.

5 To serve, dip the base of each mould quickly into hot water and run a knife around the top edge. Turn out on to serving plates and decorate with lime zest and rose petals, if using.

Step *1*

Step *3*

Step *4*

Saffron-Spiced Rice Pudding

*This rich and comforting pudding is cooked in milk delicately flavoured
with saffron and cinnamon.*

SERVES 4–5

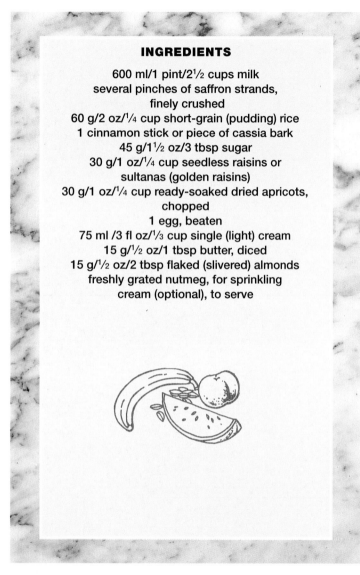

INGREDIENTS

600 ml/1 pint/2½ cups milk
several pinches of saffron strands,
finely crushed
60 g/2 oz/¼ cup short-grain (pudding) rice
1 cinnamon stick or piece of cassia bark
45 g/1½ oz/3 tbsp sugar
30 g/1 oz/¼ cup seedless raisins or
sultanas (golden raisins)
30 g/1 oz/¼ cup ready-soaked dried apricots,
chopped
1 egg, beaten
75 ml /3 fl oz/⅓ cup single (light) cream
15 g/½ oz/1 tbsp butter, diced
15 g/½ oz/2 tbsp flaked (slivered) almonds
freshly grated nutmeg, for sprinkling
cream (optional), to serve

1 Place the milk and crushed saffron in a non-stick
saucepan and bring to the boil. Stir in the rice and
cinnamon stick, reduce the heat and simmer very gently,
uncovered, for 25 minutes, stirring frequently until the
rice is tender.

2 Remove the pan from the heat and discard the
cinnamon stick. Stir in the sugar, raisins and apricots,
then beat in the egg, cream and diced butter.

3 Transfer the mixture to a greased ovenproof pie or
flan dish, sprinkle with the almonds and freshly
grated nutmeg, to taste. Place in a preheated oven,
160°C/325°F/Gas 3, for 25–30 minutes until mixture
is set and lightly golden. Serve hot with extra cream,
if wished.

Step *1*

Step *2*

Step *3*

Aromatic Fruit Salad

*The fruits in this salad are arranged attractively on serving plates
with the spicy syrup spooned over.*

SERVES 6

INGREDIENTS

45 g/1½ oz/3 tbsp sugar
150 ml/¼ pint/¾ cup water
1 cinnamon stick or large piece of cassia bark
4 cardamom pods, crushed
1 clove
juice of 1 orange
2 tbsp lime juice
½ honeydew melon
good-sized wedge of watermelon
2 ripe guavas
3 ripe nectarines
about 18 strawberries
a little toasted, shredded coconut for sprinkling
sprigs of mint or rose petals, to decorate
strained thick yogurt, to serve

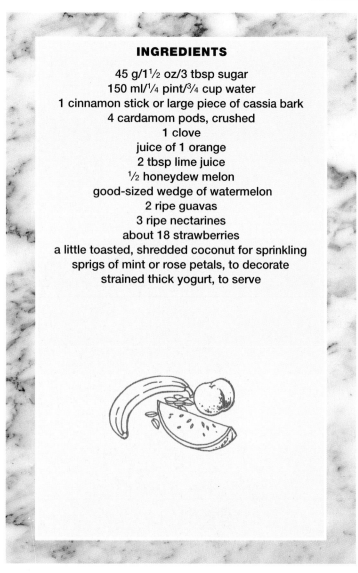

1 First prepare the syrup. Put the sugar, water, cinnamon, cardamom pods and cloves into a pan and bring to the boil, stirring to dissolve the sugar.

2 Simmer for 2 minutes, then remove from heat. Add the orange and lime juices, then leave to cool and infuse while preparing the fruits.

3 Peel and remove the seeds from the melons and cut the flesh into neat slices. Cut the guavas in half, scoop out the seeds, then peel and slice the flesh neatly. Cut the nectarines into slices, and hull and slice the strawberries.

4 Arrange the slices of fruit attractively on 6 serving plates. Strain the cooled syrup and spoon over the sliced fruits. Sprinkle with a little toasted coconut. Decorate each serving with sprigs of mint or rose petals and serve with yogurt, if wished.

Step *1*

Step *2*

Step *3*

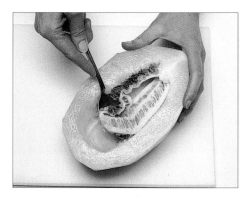

Sweet Carrot Halva

*This nutritious dessert, made from grated carrots simmered in milk,
is flavoured with spices, nuts and raisins.*

SERVES 6

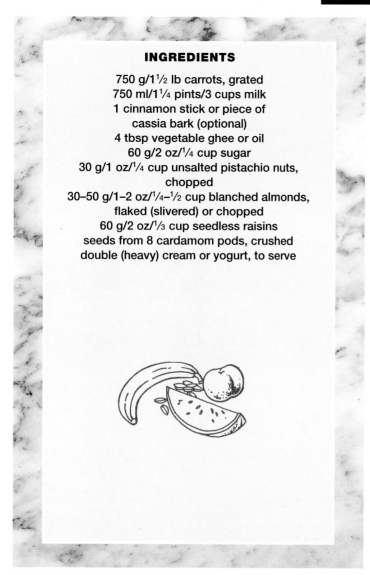

INGREDIENTS

750 g/1½ lb carrots, grated
750 ml/1¼ pints/3 cups milk
1 cinnamon stick or piece of
cassia bark (optional)
4 tbsp vegetable ghee or oil
60 g/2 oz/¼ cup sugar
30 g/1 oz/¼ cup unsalted pistachio nuts,
chopped
30–50 g/1–2 oz/¼–½ cup blanched almonds,
flaked (slivered) or chopped
60 g/2 oz/⅓ cup seedless raisins
seeds from 8 cardamom pods, crushed
double (heavy) cream or yogurt, to serve

1 Put the grated carrots, milk and cinnamon or cassia, if using, into a large, heavy-based saucepan and bring to the boil. Reduce the heat to a simmer and cook, uncovered, for 35–40 minutes, or until thickened (with no milk remaining). Stir the mixture frequently during cooking to prevent it sticking. Discard the cinnamon.

2 Heat the ghee or oil in a non-stick frying pan, add the carrot mixture and stir-fry over a medium heat for about 5 minutes or until the carrots take on a glossy sheen.

3 Add the sugar, pistachios, almonds, raisins and crushed cardamom seeds, mix well and continue frying for a further 3–4 minutes, stirring frequently. Serve warm or cold with cream or yogurt.

Step *1*

Step *2*

Step *3*

INDEX

A

ajowan *12*
almonds:
aromatic pilau *164*
  bananas with spiced yogurt and
    almonds *240*
  chicken and aromatic
    almonds *94*
  Indian ice-cream (kulfi) *246*
  lamb pasanda *102*
  Peshwari naan *210*
  spicy saffron rice *172*
  sweet carrot halva *252*
aloo chat *156*
aniseed *12*
appetizers *19–42*
apples:
  date raita *234*
  Peshwari naan *210*
apricots:
  brown rice with fruit and
    nuts *174*
aromatic basmati rice *172*
aromatic fruit salad *250*
aromatic pilau *164*
aubergines (eggplant):
  aubergine bhaji *134*
  aubergine in saffron sauce *132*
  brindil bhaji *128*
  chick-peas (garbanzo beans)
    and aubergine in tomato
    cream *196*
  lentil and vegetable biryani *178*
  mixed (bell) pepper pooris *220*
  roasted aubergine curry *130*
  spicy beef and yogurt *114*
  yellow split pea casserole *190*

B

Balti chicken paneer *86*
Balti king prawns
  jumbo shrimp) *64*
bananas:
  bananas with spiced yogurt and
    almonds *240*
  brown rice with fruit and
    nuts *174*
barbecuing *16*
basil *10*
beans *10–11*
  see also black-eyed beans; red
    kidney beans etc
beef:
  beef and mushroom curry *116*
  rogan josh *108*
  sheek kebabs *40*
  spicy beef and yogurt *114*

stuffed parathas *216*
bell peppers *see peppers*
bhagar *16*
bhajis:
  aubergine (eggplant) bhaji *134*
  bite-sized bajees *24*
  brindil bhaji *128*
  minted onion bhajis *22*
  mixed vegetable bhaji *126*
  okra bhaji *138*
  spinach and cauliflower
    bhaji *144*
bharta *16*
bhindi *see okra*
bhoona *16*
biriani:
  lamb biriani *180*
  lentil and vegetable biryani *178*
  prawn (shrimp) biriani *176*
bite-sized bajees *24*
black-eyed beans *11*
blenders *14*
breads *209–22*
  mixed (bell) pepper pooris *220*
  parathas *214*
  Peshwari naan *210*
  prawn (shrimp) pooris *218*
  spicy oven bread *212*
  spinach poori *222*
  stuffed parathas *216*
brindil bhaji *128*
broad beans (fava beans):
  chicken jalfrezi *74*
broccoli:
  spiced basmati rice *166*
brown rice with fruit and nuts *174*
butterfly prawns (shrimp) *20*

C

cardamom *12*
carrot halva, sweet *252*
cashew nuts:
  lentil and vegetable biryani *178*
  prawn (shrimp) pilau *168*
  stir-fry chicken curry *82*
  vegetable and cashew
    samosas *32*
cassia *12*
cauliflower:
  lentil and vegetable biryani *178*
  spicy cauliflower *142*
  split peas with vegetables *192*
  yellow split pea casserole *190*
cayenne pepper *12*
channa dal *11, 194*
cheese *see paneer*
chick-peas (garbanzo beans) *11*

aloo chat *156*
chick-peas and aubergine
  (eggplant) in tomato
  cream *196*
chicken with spicy chick-peas *76*
kabli channa sag *198*
chicken:
  Balti chicken paneer *86*
  chicken and aromatic
    almonds *94*
  chicken and vegetable rice *84*
  chicken in spiced coconut
    cream *88*
  chicken jalfrezi *74*
  chicken tikka masala *78*
  chicken with spicy chick-peas
    (garbanzo beans) *76*
  karahi chicken *92*
  saffron chicken *90*
  shahi murg *80*
  spiced chicken koftas with
    lime pickle *34*
  stir-fry chicken curry *82*
  tandoori chicken *72*
chillies *9, 12*
  chicken with spicy chick-peas
    (garbanzo beans) *76*
  chilli chutney *226*
  garlic chutney *228*
  lamb bhuna *112*
  lamb pasanda *102*
  lamb phall *110*
  lamb tikka masala *100*
  murkha dal *206*
  prawn (shrimp) bhuna *68*
  prawns (shrimp) and chilli
    sauce *62*
  rogan josh *108*
  tandoori chicken *72*
chutneys:
  chilli *226*
  garlic *228*
  walnut *228*
cilantro *see coriander*
cinnamon *12*
cloves *12*
coconut *9*
coconut, creamed *9*
  coconut rice *184*
coconut milk *9*
  chicken in spiced coconut
    cream *88*
  coconut ice-cream *242*
  murkha dal *206*
  prawn (shrimp) biriani *176*
  prawn (shrimp) pooris *218*
coconut oil *10*

cod:
  Indian cod with tomatoes *48*
condensed milk:
  Indian ice-cream (kulfi) *246*
coriander (cilantro) *10*
  Balti king prawns
    jumbo shrimp) *64*
  onion and tomato relish *154*
  Peshwari naan *210*
  prawn (shrimp) pilau *168*
  tarka dal *202*
  walnut chutney *228*
coriander seeds *12*
courgettes (zucchini):
  chick-peas (garbanzo beans) and
    aubergine (eggplant) in
    tomato cream *196*
  deep-fried courgettes *26*
crab, curried *60*
cream, mango and yogurt *244*
cucumber:
  cucumber raita *234*
  tomato, onion and cucumber
    kachumber *232*
cumin *12*
curd cheese *see paneer*
curry *16*
  beef and mushroom curry *116*
  chicken tikka masala *78*
  curried crab *60*
  curried okra *140*
  curried roast potatoes *152*
  egg and lentil curry *200*
  green fish curry *56*
  lamb and potato masala *104*
  lamb bhuna *112*
  lamb pasanda *102*
  lamb phall *110*
  lamb tikka masala *100*
  okra bhaji *138*
  roasted aubergine (eggplant)
    curry *130*
  rogan josh *108*
  shahi murg *80*
  shrimp curry and fruit sauce *58*
  spicy beef and yogurt *114*
  stir-fry chicken curry *82*
  vegetable curry *124*
  vindaloo curry *118*

D

dal:
  channa dal *194*
  dal with spinach *204*
  murkha dal *206*
  tarka dal *202*
date raita *234*

degchi *14*
desserts *237–52*
do pyaza *17*
dressing, yogurt *38*
drinks *8*
    lassi *8*
dry-fried spice mix *12*
dum *17*

E

eggplant *see aubergines*
eggs:
    egg and lentil curry *200*
    lentil and vegetable biryani
      178
equipment *14–15*

F

fava beans *see broad beans*
fenugreek *12*
    deep-fried battered fish *54*
fish dishes *45–68*
    green fish curry *56*
    spicy fish and potato fritters
      52
    see also cod; trout etc
food processors *14*
French beans:
    lentil and vegetable biryani *178*
fritters:
    garlicky mushroom pakoras *28*
    pakoras *30*
    potato fritters with relish *154*
    spicy fish and potato fritters *52*
fruit salad, aromatic *250*
frying pans *14*

G

garam masala *13*
garbanzo beans *see chick-peas*
garlic *9*
    garlic chutney *228*
    garlicky mushroom pakoras *28*
    lamb phall *110*
    murkha dal *206*
ghee *9–10*
ginger *10*
golden raisins *see sultanas*
gram flour *10*
    bite-sized bajees *24*
    deep-fried battered fish *54*
    minted onion bhajis *22*
grapefruit raita *234*
green beans:
    long beans with tomatoes *136*
green fish curry *56*
groundnut oil *10*

H

halva, sweet carrot *252*
herbs *10*
honey:
    bananas with spiced yogurt and
      almonds *240*
Hyderabad rice pilau *170*

I

ice-cream:
    coconut *242*
    Indian (kulfi) *246*
    mango *238*
Indian cod with tomatoes *48*
Indian grilled trout *46*
Indian ice-cream (kulfi) *246*
ingredients *9–13*

J

jumbo shrimp *see prawns*

K

kabli channa sag *198*
kachumber:
    mango *232*
    radish *232*
    tomato, onion and
      cucumber *232*
karahi *14–15*
karahi chicken *92*
Kashmiri spinach *146*
kebabs:
    butterfly prawns (shrimp) *20*
    masala kebabs *42*
    rashmi kebabs *36*
    sheek kebabs *40*
king prawns *see prawns*
kitchouri *182*
knives *15*
koftas:
    lamb and tomato *38*
    spiced chicken *34*
korma *17*
kulfi *246*

L

ladies' fingers *see okra*
lamb:
    lamb and potato masala *104*
    lamb and tomato koftas *38*
    lamb bhuna *112*
    lamb biriani *180*
    lamb do pyaza *106*
    lamb pasanda *102*
    lamb phall *110*
    lamb tikka masala *100*
    masala kebabs *42*
    masala lamb and lentils *98*
    rashmi kebabs *36*
    sheek kebabs *40*
lassi *8*
leeks:
    dal with spinach *204*
legumes *10–11*
lentils *11*
    dal with spinach *204*
    egg and lentil curry *200*
    kitchouri *182*
    lentil and vegetable biryani *178*
    masala lamb and lentils *98*
    murkha dal *206*
    prawn (shrimp) dansak *66*
    tarka dal *202*

lime:
    chilli chutney *226*
    mango ice-cream *238*
lime pickle, spiced chicken koftas
    with *34*
long beans with tomatoes *136*

M

mangoes:
    mango and yogurt cream *244*
    mango ice-cream *238*
    mango kachumber *232*
marinating *17*
masala fried fish *50*
masala kebabs *42*
masala lamb and lentils *98*
masala sauce, lamb tikka
    masala *100*
meat dishes *97–120*
meatballs:
    lamb and tomato koftas *38*
    spiced chicken koftas with lime
      pickle *34*
melon raita *234*
milk:
    paneer *158*
    saffron-spiced rice pudding *248*
    sweet carrot halva *252*
mint *10*
    mint and yogurt relish *222*
    minted onion bhajis *22*
murkha dal *206*
mushrooms:
    beef and mushroom curry *116*
    chicken in spiced coconut
      cream *88*
    garlicky mushroom pakoras *28*
    lamb and potato masala *104*
    lentil and vegetable biryani *178*
    spiced basmati rice *166*
    split peas with vegetables *192*
mussel morsels *26*
mustard oil *10*
mustard seeds *13*
muttar paneer *158*

N

naan, Peshwari *210*
Northern India *6*
nuts *10*
    brown rice with fruit and
      nuts *174*
    spiced nuts *26*
    *see also almonds; pistachio
      nuts etc*

O

oils *10*
okra:
    curried okra *140*
    Hyderabad rice pilau *170*
    okra bhaji *138*
onion seeds *13*
onions:
    bite-sized bajees *24*

fried spiced potatoes *150*
    lamb do pyaza *106*
    minted onion bhajis *22*
    onion and tomato relish *154*
    tomato, onion and cucumber
      kachumber *232*
oven bread, spicy *212*

P

pakoras *30*
    garlicky mushroom pakoras *28*
palak paneer *160*
panch poran spice mix *134*
paneer *158*
    Balti chicken paneer *86*
    muttar paneer *158*
    palak paneer *160*
paprika *13*
parathas *214*
    stuffed parathas *216*
parsley *10*
pastries:
    vegetable and cashew
      samosas *32*
peanuts:
    garlic chutney *228*
peas:
    aromatic pilau *164*
    brown rice with fruit and
      nuts *174*
    muttar paneer *158*
    split peas with vegetables *192*
    stuffed parathas *216*
peas, split *see split peas*
peppercorns *13*
peppers (bell):
    brown rice with fruit and
      nuts *174*
    chicken jalfrezi *74*
    dal with spinach *204*
    lentil and vegetable biryani *178*
    mixed pepper pooris *220*
    okra bhaji *138*
    rashmi kebabs *36*
    stir-fry chicken curry *82*
Peshwari naan *210*
pestle and mortar *15*
pilau:
    aromatic pilau *164*
    Hyderabad rice pilau *170*
    prawn (shrimp) pilau *168*
pineapple:
    melon raita *234*
pistachio nuts:
    Indian ice-cream (kulfi) *246*
    spiced basmati rice *166*
    sweet carrot halva *252*
plaice:
    deep-fried battered fish *54*
    masala fried fish *50*
pooris:
    mixed (bell) pepper pooris *220*
    prawn (shrimp) pooris *218*
    spinach poori *222*
poppy seeds *13*

pork:
    pork chops and spicy red
      beans *120*
    vindaloo curry *118*
potatoes:
    aloo chat *156*
    curried roast potatoes *152*
    fried spiced potatoes *150*
    lamb and potato masala *104*
    palak paneer *160*
    potato fritters with relish *154*
    spicy fish and potato fritters *52*
    spicy Indian-style potatoes *148*
    split peas with vegetables *192*
poultry dishes *71–94*
prawns (shrimp):
    Balti king prawns
      (jumbo shrimp) *64*
    butterfly prawns *20*
    prawn bhuna *68*
    prawn biriani *176*
    prawn dansak *66*
    prawn pilau *168*
    prawn pooris *218*
    prawns and chilli sauce *62*
    shrimp curry and fruit sauce *58*
pulses *10–11, 189–206*
pumpkin:
    yellow split pea casserole *190*

R

radish kachumber *232*
raisins:
    aromatic pilau *164*
    shrimp curry and fruit sauce
      58
    sweet carrot halva *252*
raisins, golden *see sultanas*
raita:
    cucumber *234*
    date *234*
    grapefruit *234*
    melon *234*
rashmi kebabs *36*
red kidney beans *11*
    pork chops and spicy red
      beans *120*
relishes:
    mint and yogurt *222*
    onion and tomato *154*
rice *11, 163–86*
    aromatic basmati rice *172*
    aromatic pilau *164*
    brown rice with fruit and
      nuts *174*
    chicken and vegetable rice *84*
    coconut rice *184*
    Hyderabad rice pilau *170*
    kitchouri *182*
    lamb biriani *180*
    lentil and vegetable biryani *178*
    prawn (shrimp) biriani *176*
    prawn (shrimp) pilau *168*
    saffron rice *186*
    saffron-spiced rice pudding *248*

spiced basmati rice *166*
spicy saffron rice *172*
rogan josh *108*
rose water *11*

S

saffron *13*
    aubergine (eggplant) in saffron
      sauce *132*
    bananas with spiced yogurt and
      almonds *240*
    saffron chicken *90*
    saffron rice *186*
    saffron-spiced rice pudding *248*
    spicy saffron rice *172*
salads:
    aloo chat *156*
    mango kachumber *232*
    radish kachumber *232*
    tomato, onion and cucumber
      kachumber *232*
samosas, vegetable and cashew *32*
saucepans *15*
sauces:
    masala *100*
    prawns (shrimp) and chilli *62*
scallions *see spring onions*
sesame oil *10*
shahi murg *80*
sheek kebabs *40*
shrimp *see prawns*
skewers *15*
skillets *14*
Southern India *6–8*
spiced basmati rice *166*
spiced chicken koftas with lime
    pickle *34*
spiced nuts *26*
spices *12*
    dry-fried spice mix *12*
    panch poran spice mix *134*
spicy beef and yogurt *114*
spicy bites *26*
spicy cauliflower *142*
spicy fish and potato fritters *52*
spicy Indian-style potatoes *148*
spicy oven bread *212*
spicy saffron rice *172*
spinach:
    dal with spinach *204*
    kabli channa sag *198*
    Kashmiri spinach *146*
    palak paneer *160*
    prawn (shrimp) pooris *218*
    spinach and cauliflower
      bhaji *144*
    spinach poori *222*
split peas:
    channa dal *194*
    split peas with vegetables *192*
    yellow split pea casserole
      190
spring onions (scallions):
    coconut rice *184*
    curried okra *140*

mussel morsels *26*
    potato fritters with relish *154*
sultanas (golden raisins):
    Hyderabad rice pilau *170*
    Peshwari naan *210*
sunflower oil *10*
sweet carrot halva *252*
sweetcorn:
    potato fritters with relish *154*

T

talawa *17*
tamarind *13*
tandoori chicken *72*
tarka dal *202*
tava *15*
techniques *16–17*
thali *15*
tomatoes:
    aubergine (eggplant) bhaji *134*
    brindil bhaji *128*
    brown rice with fruit and
      nuts *174*
    channa dal *194*
    chick-peas (garbanzo beans) and
      aubergine (eggplant) in
      tomato cream *196*
    chicken tikka masala *78*
    egg and lentil curry *200*
    Indian cod with tomatoes *48*
    lamb and tomato koftas *38*
    lamb phall *110*
    lamb tikka masala *100*
    lentil and vegetable biryani *178*
    long beans with tomatoes *136*
    mixed (bell) pepper pooris *220*
    muttar paneer *158*
    onion and tomato relish *154*
    palak paneer *160*
    prawn (shrimp) dansak *66*
    prawn (shrimp) pooris *218*
    shrimp curry and fruit sauce *58*
    spinach and cauliflower
      bhaji *144*
    split peas with vegetables *192*
    tarka dal *202*
    tomato, onion and cucumber
      kachumber *232*
    yellow split pea casserole *190*
tongs *15*
trout, Indian grilled *46*
turmeric *13*

V

vark *13*
vegetables *123–60*
    chicken and vegetable rice *84*
    lentil and vegetable biryani *178*
    mixed vegetable bhaji *126*
    pakoras *30*
    split peas with vegetables *192*
    vegetable and cashew samosas *32*
    vegetable curry *124*
    see also potatoes; spinach etc
vindaloo curry *118*

W

walnut chutney *228*

Y

yellow split pea casserole *190*
yogurt *13*
    aloo chat *156*
    bananas with spiced yogurt and
      almonds *240*
    bite-sized bajees *24*
    cucumber raita *234*
    curried crab *60*
    date raita *234*
    fried spiced potatoes *150*
    grapefruit raita *234*
    lamb biriani *180*
    lamb pasanda *102*
    lamb tikka masala *100*
    lassi *8*
    mango and yogurt cream *244*
    melon raita *234*
    mint and yogurt relish *222*
    minted onion bhajis *22*
    prawn (shrimp) biriani *176*
    roasted aubergine (eggplant)
      curry *130*
    shahi murg *80*
    spicy beef and yogurt *114*
    tandoori chicken *72*
    walnut chutney *228*
    yogurt dressing *38*

Z

zucchini *see courgettes*